Language, ignorance and education

Explorations in Language Study

Literary Text and Language Study
Ronald Carter and Deirdre Burton, editors

Assessing Writing: Principles and Practice of Marking Written English
Peter Gannon

Explorations in the Functions of Language
M.A.K. Halliday

Learning How to Mean – Explorations in the Development of Language
M.A.K. Halliday

Language Projects
S. Harris and K. Morgan

English as a Second and Foreign Language
Brian Harrison

The Resources of Classroom Language
John Richmond

They Don't Speak our Language – Essays on the Language World of
   Children and Adolescents
Sinclair Rogers, editor

Language in Bilingual Communities
Derrick Sharp

Language, Experience and School
Geoffrey Thornton

Teaching Writing: The Development of Written Language Skills
Geoffrey Thornton

Accent, Dialect and the School
Peter Trudgill

Explorations in Language Study
General Editors
Peter Doughty   Geoffrey Thornton

LANGUAGE, IGNORANCE AND EDUCATION

Geoffrey Thornton

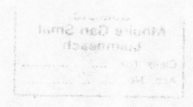

EDWARD ARNOLD

First published in Great Britain 1986 by
Edward Arnold (Publishers) Ltd, 41 Bedford Square, London WC1B 3DQ

Edward Arnold (Australia) Pty Ltd, 80 Waverley Road, Caulfield East,
  Victoria 3145, Australia

Edward Arnold, 3 East Read Street, Baltimore, Maryland 21202, USA

British Library Cataloguing in Publication Data
Thornton, Geoffrey
  Language, ignorance and education. ——
  (Explorations in language study)
  1. Language and education
  I. Title   II. Series
  370   P40.8

  ISBN 0-7131-6481-6

Text set in 11/13 pt Baskerville Compugraphic
by Colset Private Ltd, Singapore
Printed and bound by Richard Clay Plc, Bungay.

Contents

		Page
General Introduction		1
Foreword		3
Introduction		5
1	Linguistic 'flat-earthers'	11
2	Graded nonsense	19
3	'Needs urgent attention'	33
4	What do teachers need to know about language?	43
5	'Delivering the curriculum'	51
6	Delivering the goods	57
7	'Wot's it all for?'	67
References		79
A note on reading		81
Appendix		83

General Introduction

In the course of our efforts to develop a linguistic focus for work in English language, which was published as *Language in Use*, we came to realize the extent of the growing interest in what we would call a linguistic approach to language. Lecturers in Colleges and Departments of Education see the relevance of such an approach in the education of teachers. Many teachers in schools and in Colleges of Further Education recognize that 'educational failure is primarily *linguistic* failure', and are turning to Linguistic Science for some kind of exploration and practical guidance. Many of those now exploring the problems of relationships, community or society, from a sociological or psychological point of view wish to make use of a linguistic approach to the language in so far as it is relevant to these problems.

We were conscious of the wide divergence between the aims of the linguist, primarily interested in describing language as a system for organizing 'meanings', and the needs of those who now wanted to gain access to the insights that resulted from that interest. In particular, we were aware of the wide gap that separated the literature of academic Linguistics from the majority of those who wished to find out what Linguistic Science might have to say about language and the use of language.

Out of this experience emerged our own view of that much-used term, 'Language Study', developed initially in the chapters of *Exploring Language*, and now given expression in this series. Language Study is not a subject, but a process, which is why the series is called *Explorations in Language Study*. Each exploration is focused upon a meeting point between the insights of

1

Linguistic Science, often in conjunction with other social sciences, and the linguistic questions raised by the study of a particular aspect of individual behaviour or human society.

The volumes in this series have a particular relevance to the role of language in teaching and learning. The editors intend that they should make a basic contribution to the literature of Language Study, doing justice equally to the findings of the academic discipline involved and the practical need of those who now want to take a linguistic view of their own particular problems of language and the use of language.

Peter Doughty
Geoffrey Thornton

I should like to acknowledge, and record my gratitude for, the help given by Peter Doughty in enabling me to turn my first draft into a book.

Geoffrey Thornton

Foreword

T.Crews
has to inform the overseers of St Martins that is apprentice
John Marshall his this day accuainted him he his 21 yrs of age
when Bound he was stated to be Thirteen or thereabouts he
has not yet served 7 yrs T.C. fears he had bad advisers which
no doubt the Overseers will take care off he verry much
doubts him to be 21 yrs.

This book is not an autobiography, but in the writing of it I
have drawn heavily on my experience since I started teaching
English in 1950. After seventeen years as a teacher, I spent four
years as a member of the Schools Council Programme in Linguistics and English Teaching, and then twelve as an English
Adviser/Inspector, six in Cheshire and six in the ILEA.

I have put at the head of this Foreword a note that I found
pinned to a page of the Register of Apprentices in the Parish of
St Martin's, London, for the year 1815. Problems caused by
some aspects of the English writing system do not change, even
if we inhabit a different world from that of Mr Crews. The name
of my great-great-grandfather appeared on the page of the Register to which the note was pinned. He was apprenticed in 1815,
at the age of ten, together with five other children of similar age,
to one David Ainsworth, owner of the Backbarrow Mills, near
Cartmel. He ended his days in Tissington, Derbyshire, as a
'book-keeper and overlooker' in the mill at Fenny Bentley
nearby. He had, at some stage, learned to read and write.

One of his great-grandsons was my father, himself a teacher,
the third and last Headmaster of the Edward Worlledge Central

School in Great Yarmouth, before it was abolished by the 1944 Education Act. When he died, in the year in which I began teaching, he was, as an elected Councillor, a member of the Education Committee. We can therefore claim between us seventy-five years unbroken service. It gives a kind of perspective.

Introduction

This book is born out of the conviction that the English curriculum in our secondary schools (and by curriculum I mean both content and process, the what and the how) is still, despite the vast amount of work that has gone into improving it in the last twenty-five years, not operating to the maximum advantage of those for whom, and for whom alone, it exists – the pupils in our schools. This conviction is accompanied by a profound irritation at the failure, during the same period, to create an intellectual climate within which fruitful change might be brought about.

There is now a large body of research evidence attesting to the correlation between the socio-economic background from which children come and their potential for success within our education system. Those pupils in greatest need do not always receive effective help, especially in the most crucial area of all – that of language. It is a central argument of the book that teachers, on the whole, and many of those concerned with the running of an education system, lack a necessary intellectual framework, one which includes an adequate model of language, what it is, and how it works. Language Study, as a major and obligatory element in all courses for those training to be teachers, at whatever level in the system they intend to work, and whatever their specialism might be, has still not achieved the status that Bullock called for over ten years ago.

Apart from this, it has to be said, as Professor M.A.K. Halliday pointed out nearly ten years ago, in his Introduction to the first of the Papers produced by the Programme in Linguistics and English Teaching,[1] that we live in a culture 'lacking in linguistic sympathy'. This manifest itself most noticeably in the licence people allow themselves to comment disparagingly and authoritatively on the way in which other people speak and write.

The custom has a long tradition. During the course of my researches into my forbears, I looked at the life and works of the Rev. John Thornton, of Billericay. (He turned out to be no relation.) He was born near Wakefield in 1776, and entered into an apprenticeship in Saddleworth, near Oldham, in 1792. Five years later he went south, to study for the Congregational Ministry at Hoxton Academy. He took up his Ministry in Billericay, where he lived for the rest of his life. He became something of an author, writing, among other works, a book with the splendid title, *Serious Warnings Addressed to Various Classes of Persons*. In a book published in 1830, he wrote,

> Perhaps there is no part of England where the provincial dialect is so bad as in Saddleworth, and as I had lived entirely among the lower class my pronunciation was miserably uncouth and repulsive.

In his book *Tuscan Retreat*, published long after this, in 1964, Vernon Bartlett wrote,

> I hate the British – no, in this case, definitely the English – system of education. By perpetuating a privilege of accents, such as I have never found in any other country, it robs millions of Englishman of equality of opportunity and their country of a great deal of ability.

It is not as if there have been no voices speaking out against this tradition, and warning of its implications for education. One example may suffice, because of the way, as far back as 1910, the author had fastened on the consequences for children's education of attitudes towards the way in which they speak.

In that year, the Priory Press in Hampstead published a sixpenny pamphlet called 'London's Dialect' by Mac Kenzie Mac Bride. The first chapter had originally appeared in the

6

London Evening News, after Mr Mac Bride had been provoked by the publication of a 'Report of the Conference on the Teaching of English in London Elementary Schools.' The Conference had been sponsored by the Education Department of the London County Council in the previous year. The article began by quoting from the report.

It must not be forgotten that London has a special responsibility for the maintenance of a satisfactory standard of English as a spoken or a literary medium. Many of the so-called provincial dialects are. . . . survivals of older forms of the language, and are thus historically and phonetically justified. When a boy or girl in Devonshire, Lincolnshire, or Yorkshire is taught to acquire the construction of the King's English at the expense of his native forms of speech, there is a balance of loss and gain in the process. But with the pupil in the London elementary school this is not the case. The Cockney mode of speech, with its unpleasant twang, is a modern corruption without legitimate credentials, and is unworthy of being the speech of any person in the capital city of the Empire. There, if anywhere, the endeavour should be made to diffuse as widely as possible the standard English which, as the result of a long process of development, has become the normal national means of expression.

Mr Mac Bride's comment on that was robust.

This is an astounding statement, and one which I hope to show is entirely without foundation in historical fact; such a thing as a dialect which, in the words of the report, has 'no reputable antecedents and origin,' and which is not 'a survival of older forms of the language and thus historically and phonetically justified,' does not exist.

Dialects are not deliberately invented; they do not come up in the night like mushrooms. Speech is determined by natural tendencies, or unconscious local preferences, or by other dialects or languages. Even in the case of deliberate affectations of speech such as the 'haw haw' dialect of the would-be aristocrats of England, of 'Kelvinside', or of Edinburgh, new forms are seldom, if ever, made. People merely imitate some form already in existence in another dialect of the same tongue which they think to be more refined than the speech of their fathers.

Curiously enough, there is no place in the kingdom more local than London: it is only cosmopolitan in its great and admirable tolerance of strangers.

He explores some of the educational implications in his next chapter, pointing out what he takes to be an essential contradiction in the Report:

. . . . the Conference say they 'are aware that educational investigators unite in deploring the initial poverty of vocabulary and the absence of facility in its employment among our chilldren and emphasise their almost universal resort to monosyllabic responses and broken phrases in framing answers even to the simplest questions. But,' they add, 'a little child has a by no means meagre store of elementary ideas, and he certainly possesses a vivid imagination and active powers of invention. Moreover, his inability to express himself fluently and promptly is no proof of absence of word material, or of a stock of sense experiences.' . . . . . 'It would appear,' they add sagely, 'the more effective method to utilise – rather than ignore – the potentialities of this already existing stock of material, by training him to narrate in his own words the most interesting experiences of his own active life.'

All this is a roundabout way of saying a very obvious thing which should have been realised long ago – that in training a child you must use the language a child knows, and not attempt to teach English to Welsh children by means of teachers who don't know Welsh, or English to Highland children by means of teachers who don't know Gaelic, or to London children by persons who wish to root up the only dialect the children understand. They are, moreover, ignorant of its history and origin, and, worst of all, allow the children to see that they despise it. They themselves say:-

'In London. . . . the circumstances are unique. We have to face an importation or corruption in the form of Cockneyism which has been in use for several generations, and which, notwithstanding the Education Acts, appears to be still flourishing. Most dialects have their own distinctive

8

charm and historical interest, but Cockneyism seems to have no redeeming features and needs only to be heard to be condemned.'

Mr Mac Bride comments on this,

To be taught by a person who holds such views as these of the dialect we speak can only stultify the minds of the children and result in young people giving answers in the fewest words possible.

We are still, seventy-five years on, having to fight the same battle as Mr Mac Bride. It is not yet universally acknowledged that, if you do not allow children in school to speak their own language, the language they have grown up with, the only language they know, then, effectively, you do not allow them to speak at all. If you do not allow them to speak, you are cutting them off from the educational process.

There still appear in the press letters about dialects no different in substance and tone from what was being said by the Education Department of the LCC during and after its Conference in 1909. Statements of the same kind are also quite likely to figure in articles by the latest gurus, say on the back page of the *Times Educational Supplement*, where there never seems to be a reluctance to reveal what, in the next chapter, will be discussed as a 'flat-earth' view of language. Thus we have Paul Johnson, in the *TES* of 17 January, 1986, with the effortless ease of the invincibly ignorant, in a piece regretting the failure to teach pupils in school nowadays how to write essays, declaring that, compared with English, 'Of course, French is an easier language to spell and write – and indeed pronounce – once you know the rules.'

Of such is the stock-in-trade of linguistic 'flat-earthers'.

1 Linguistic 'flat-earthers'

In the Autumn of 1984, the DES published a document called *English from 5–16*, the first of a series titled, archly, 'Curriculum Matters'. It was totally predictable that press comments should, almost in their entirety, focus on the fact that the document mentioned 'Parts of Speech', setting as objectives for pupils of 11 that they should know, among other things, 'The functions and names of the main parts of speech (noun, pronoun, verb, adjective and adverb) . . .' while 16-year-olds should know the names and functions of *all* the main parts of speech, adding article, preposition and conjunction to their repertoire during the five years of secondary schooling.

It was predictable, because most journalists who write on educational matters, like the vast majority of the population at large, remain 'linguistic flat-earthers' at heart. Just as astronomers before Copernicus believed that the sun revolved round the earth, so most people retain the belief that language revolves round the Parts of Speech. Any scientific view of language, that is, a description of what it is and how it works, based upon the work of linguists in this century, especially after the second world war, has completely failed to penetrate the cultural background. Many publishers' lists now contains works by linguists which give accessible accounts of contemporary linguistic studies. Nevertheless, a naive linguistic model still occupies a place at the centre of most people's thinking about language.

Giving Parts of Speech a quasi-religious status in language is a hallmark of the flat-earth view of language, but there are other superstitious beliefs as well. A corollary to that about Parts of

Speech is the notion that meaning resides wholly in words, which are seen as simple building blocks. There is much more to language than words, and more to meaning than just putting words together. In speech there is a whole repertoire of devices available to the speaker – intonation, gesture, pausing, etc.

Attitudes to the way in which other people speak have been discussed in the Introduction, and these may extend to the idea that speech itself is but a debased form of writing. This often betrays itself in an appeal to the written form for authority on how to pronounce a word, or even the assertion that one should pronounce every letter. (One reply to that might be, 'Good night!) There is, too, a whole rag-bag of shibboleths about the notion of 'correctness', including split infinitives and ending sentences with prepositions. Many of these have to do with a mistaken conception of 'grammar', dealt with by Frank Palmer in his book.[1] As he points out, such misconceptions include the idea that a grammar of a language is a book written about it; that grammar is found only in the written language, not the spoken; that some languages (e.g. Latin) have grammar and some do not; that grammar may be good or bad; and that some people know the grammar of their own language while others do not. Anybody who can put together a grammatical structure, that is, a stretch of language capable of conveying meaning, knows something about the grammar of that language, even if he/she cannot make that knowledge explicit. As Professor Palmer says, grammar 'describes what people do when they speak; it is not something that has to be found in books, written down or learnt by heart.'

Misconceptions about the nature of grammar lead to a cluster of beliefs about the way in which children acquire language in infancy, and learn to extend their ability to use it. These beliefs have to do with the age at which children start to acquire language, and what are the signs of linguistic development. First sounds are often hailed with enthusiasm, as if language has suddenly begun at that point in time. A great deal of understanding of language has been laid down before recognizable linguistic sounds are uttered – this is obvious from the way in which even small babies respond to the language of adults. They can begin to decode it before they begin to use it for themselves. The acquisition of language is a process beginning almost from birth, and one that may continue to the end of one's life. Children grow, and their language grows with them. They do not need to be taught the Parts of Speech in the cradle. The human brain gives us the capacity to sort out for ourselves the rules of the language used in the environment into which we are born, so that we come naturally (if we have a normal brain, that is) to understand and speak that language.

It may be that a mistaken view of the process of initial acquisition will lead, in the end, to the supposition that language development in school requires some 'teachable content', such as the dictation of grammatical rules, or rules for the use of stops. Bound up with this may well be a notion that development proceeds upon some kind of linear path. One implication of that belief will form the subject of the next chapter.

Perhaps the most disturbing feature of the persistence of a 'flat-earth' view of language so deeply embedded in our culture is that it may be held by some who occupy influential positions in the world of education. In some universities there are chairs of 'Language and Literature', although, apart perhaps from Anglo-Saxon, it is not always immediately obvious what the word 'language' in the designation refers to. It is almost (to pursue the analogy with astronomy) as if there coexisted in Universities two departments: one based upon a Copernican astronomy, and one based upon a thought-world in which the sun forever circles the earth. In the same way, side by side with departments of Linguistics, in which language is studied on a scientific, observable, describable basis, there exist departments of Literature, or Language and Literature, in which facts of language are displaced by myths. To such myths, the name 'folk-linguistics' has been given; they are a kind of folk-lore.

To the flat-earther, anything to do with language is apparantly simple, any problems capable of easy solution. Thus we are liable to have papers published by organizations like the National Council for Educational Standards, calling grandly for this and that, written by authors who seemingly cannot handle basic linguistic concepts like grammar and lexis, or accent and dialect. One can hear, or read reports from, people working with young people in capacities as various as Drama Advisers or Child Psychiatrist complaining about 'slovenly' or 'careless' speech.[2]

> . . . some of his speech was so careless that I had difficulty in understanding him. The shape of some of his words was corrupt and it would appear that this boy has a severe verbal defect which will handicap him badly.

With a woolly diagnosis like that, what chance has the boy? What chance, either, will teachers have on a course for an Advanced Diploma in Educational Studies, the Education of Children with Special Needs, run by a University Institute of Education, when, in the pamphlet describing the course, the first sentence under the heading The Development of Writing begins,

> The automatization of secretarial skills of spelling, handwriting, punctuation and grammar . . .

If those who run the course conceive of writing in such naive terms, and pass on their view to teachers, what chance indeed will the Special Needs of their pupils stand of being met?

It is interesting to speculate on the reasons for the failure of an intellectually reputable view of language to establish itself in the culture. After all, the ideas of Freud enshrined themselves with some rapidity in the twenties and thirties. What are the influences that have led to the persistent rejection of ideas about language based upon observation and evidence in favour of the retention of demonstrably false beliefs? One such influence can, I think, be ascribed to the study of Classics in Public Schools and Universities, a study which bequeathed mistaken emphases on Greek and Latin grammar and on the status of written texts, which constituted the only available corpus of evidence. When English Literature emerged as a subject for University study in the late nineteenth century, it seems to have been assumed that, as far as language, and its structure were concerned, Latin was the key. Knowledge *about* Latin, which nobody had spoken for

14

many centuries, was essential for anyone presuming to call himself a 'man of letters'. (There were, in those days, no – or hardly any – 'women of letters')

The view taken of grammar in the second half of the nineteenth century may be seen from the title page of a book called *A Manual of Our Mother Tongue* by Hewitt and Beach, the fifth edition published in 1889.

A MANUAL

OF

OUR MOTHER TONGUE.

CONTAINING A COMPLETE ACCIDENCE AND SYNTAX,
CHAPTERS ON ANALYSIS, PARSING, COMPOSITION, PARAPHRASING, ETC.,
WORD-BUILDING AND DERIVATION,
A SKETCH OF THE HISTORY OF THE ENGLISH TONGUE,
TABLE OF AUTHORS,
NOTES ON THE STUDY OF WORDS,
AN OUTLINE OF ANGLO-SAXON GRAMMAR,
HINTS ON BEHAVIOUR IN EXAMINATION,
AND
A VOCABULARY OF INTERESTING ETYMOLOGIES.

WITH A LARGE APPARATUS OF ANSWERED AND UNANSWERED
QUESTIONS (FOR THE USE OF STUDENTS),
A COMPLETE COLLECTION OF THE PAPERS DURING
THIRTEEN YEARS OF THE LONDON UNIVERSITY
MATRICULATION EXAMINATION, AND
UPWARDS OF THIRTY PAPERS RECENTLY SET BY THE VICTORIA
UNIVERSITY, THE EDUCATION DEPARTMENT, AND THE
COLLEGE OF PRECEPTORS.

BY

H. MARMADUKE HEWITT, M.A., LL.M.,

LATE ASSISTANT-EXAMINER IN THE UNIVERSITY OF LONDON,
FOR MANY YEARS AN EXAMINER IN THE CAMBRIDGE 'LOCAL' AND
'SCHOOLS' SYNDICATE' EXAMINATIONS ;

AND

GEORGE BEACH, M.A., LL.D.

FIFTH EDITION.

LONDON: JOSEPH HUGHES,
PILGRIM STREET, LUDGATE HILL, E.C.
1889.

Its purpose is clear from the collections of examination papers included at the end, English Language Papers from London Matriculation Exams, from the College of Preceptors Pupils' Examinations, and First, Second, Third and Fourth Year Pupil Teachers' Questions (Males and Females). Candidates are required to parse, to analyse, to define, to write out tenses, to discuss the meaning and use of final syllables, to paraphrase, to explain and illustrate (as to a class) the meaning of grammatical terms like relative, imperative, potential, passive, intransitive and irregular. All the quotations for parsing, analysis, paraphrase are taken from literature. The authors would no doubt claim that all the knowledge needed by candidates for these exams is contained in the 800-odd pages of their book. (There is a section entitled 'Examples of Bad Grammar', with corrections given towards the end of the book. No. 55 in a list of 173 examples is 'How sweet the moonlight sleeps upon this bank.' According to the correction, Shakespeare should have written, 'How sweetly the moonlight sleeps upon this bank.')

The book starts with four pages of definitions, in which Grammar is defined as 'the sum total of the rules and principles by which Language is guided', and is divided into six parts: orthography (the proper mode of writing and spelling words); orthoepy (the science of correct pronunciation); etymology (which includes the classification into parts of speech); syntax (the arrangement of words in sentences and the combination of sentences); prosody (the laws of versification); and accidence (the study of forms). Part I is concerned with Parts of Speech, Part II with the syntax of parts of speech. Together, they take up nearly half the book. This view of the importance of the parts of speech retains its place in our mental furniture, despite the wholly different perspective on language that scientific observation of the phenomenon has given us, and despite the palpable fact that the definitions traditionally attached to them constitute an intellectual nonsense. This is made clear by Frank Palmer. The definitions known by most people begin, 'A noun is the name of a person, place or thing, and a verb is a doing word.' These are the definitions used by Nesfield in his *Manual of English Grammar and Comprehension*, which was published in 1898, and was destined to play an influential part in the endurance in our culture and in our education system, like a virus immune to intellectual attack, of such notional definitions of the parts of speech. How, asks Palmer, 'do we know what a thing is? Is fire a thing? Is peace? Is hope or intention? Moreover, can we not say that *red* is the name of a colour and is not *red* then a noun? Nesfield talks about qualities as things but one would normally think that the words for qualities were adjectives – *brave, foolish, good,* etc.'

Definitions which merely indicate, vaguely and imprecisely, what words refer to in the world outside, and say nothing about the *grammatical* characteristics of the word (e.g. A noun is a word which can act as the subject of a sentence and be preceded by a, an, the, this/that and words like them) are less than helpful. Indeed, it has been said that such definitions only work if you already know the answer. Thus, if a verb is a 'doing word' why, in the sentence, 'Grandma had one of her queer turns yesterday', is 'turns' not a verb? It is the only 'doing word' there. It is a noun, but of what kind of thing is it the name?

Yet, despite the intellectual sogginess of such definitions, they are the ones that still appear in course books, that pupils still copy into the exercise books (sometimes at the beginning of every year in secondary school), and that people have in mind when they write, or react to, publications like *English from 5–16*.

How to account for the persistence, at what must be called the highest levels of our intellectual life, of such a 'flat-earth view' of language? How can the evidence be so ignored? Sir Peter Medawar, in *The Art of the Solube*, quotes William Whewell, in his *Philosophy of the Inductive Sciences*, published in 1840:

Facts cannot be observed as Facts except in virtue of the conceptions which the observer unconsciously supplies.

What is the nature of the conceptions that have prevented so many from recognizing the facts of language? In 1950, the Historical Association published a pamphlet, by Angus Armitage, called *Copernicus and the Reformation of Astronomy*. The author began by noting how, 'During the past four centuries, the processes of nature have come to be viewed in a new light through the *progressive acquisition of the systematized, verifiable knowledge that we call science.'* (My italics)

He discusses how, for long, 'the central position in the Universe was assigned to the Earth, round which all the heavenly bodies were thought to revolve', adding, 'This conclusion was dictated, partly by the direct testimony of the senses, and partly by a philosophy of nature which was itself based upon superficial observations of how things behave, or even upon pre-conceptions as to how they ought to behave.'

Mutatis mutandis, it is a statement precisely applicable to the way in which a pre-scientific, a 'folk-linguistic', view of language has continued to occupy its 'central position' because people do not want to dethrone it. It suits their preconceptions of what ought to be. They are quite willing to accept the educational implications, such as the continued reliance on ineffective teaching methods, but do not appear to understand that this is the fundamental cause of a situation about which they complain. Initiatives which purport to remedy the situation are constantly being proposed, but are doomed to failure because they address the symptoms without looking for their cause. The latest, and perhaps most potentially damaging in its implications, because they are so widespread, is Graded Tests. Rarely can a scheme with such far-reaching consequences have been launched on such a slender intellectual foundation, and with so little prior discussion and investigation. The initiative forms the subject of the next chapter.

2 Graded nonsense

On Friday, 5 November, 1982, the main item on the front page of the *Times Educational Supplement* had two headlines:

ILEA and Exam Boards await green light on scheme for English and Maths

Graded Tests for London

The first two paragraphs of the article read:

Two examining Boards and the country's biggest education authority are poised to collaborate in a unique initiative to introduce graded tests in English and mathematics.

The scheme is being worked out between the Inner London Education Authority, the University Entrance and Schools Examination Council of the University of London, and the London Regional Examining Board.

A subsequent paragraph says that 'the tests will be made available to young school leavers and adults who want an objective and accepted measure of their competence in numeracy and literacy.'

In this way, notice was served that the Graded Tests bandwagon was about to roll. Soon there were to be groups of people, up and down the country, feverishly trying to work out criteria for Graded Tests, although the word 'tests' did not survive for long. (It is interesting to note that Schools Council Examinations Bulletin 41, published in 1982, was Andrew Harrison's 'Review of graded tests', and consisted largely of an account of the use being made of graded tests by teachers of

French.) However, as the naivety of the original suggestion became apparent, the term 'Graded Assessment' gained currency, in accordance with the long-established principle, 'When in difficulty, raise the level of generalization.'

Two fundamental questions need (or, rather, needed) to be asked about the concept. Is some form of Graded Assessment desirable? If so, is it feasible? As far as English is concerned, the essential difficulty in the way of giving a positive answer to either question arises from the nature of language itself, above all from its complexity. This embraces the complexity of its structure and functional nature, of what it is as a human attribute and the part that it plays in human life. From what we know of the way in which it is learnt in infancy, and of how the ability to use it is extended, it is a phenomenon not readily susceptible of being cut up into assessable segments, or delivered in teachable instalments. That this was not clearly understood by the original proponents of the scheme was signalled by the decision to make English and Mathematics the twin starting-points, as if they were sufficiently similar in content and teaching methods to be equally susceptible of the 'graded treatment'. Perhaps, too, it was thought that there was a sufficient similarity between English and French, being taught as a foreign language, for the experimental use of Graded Tests in French to contain relevant lessons. Be that as it may, the reference in the *TES* article to pupils being offered 'an objective and accepted measure of their competence in numeracy and literacy' presumes that this could be established in the same way in both subjects.

The fact is that, before the decision to go ahead with Graded Tests in English was taken, no advice was sought as to its feasibility on linguistic grounds. Moreover, when various working parties were established to work on the definition of criteria, whether at national level (e.g. the Secondary Examinations Council's working party) or at local level (e.g. regional examining boards) a linguistic perspective was inadequately represented.

Now, after three years work, draft proposals are beginning to see the light of day, and it is becoming possible to comment on their surface features and to glimpse some of the underlying assumptions.

One proposal envisaged the assessment of competences, with competence defined as 'a quality of performance which a successful language-user must be able to demonstrate'. It is explained that, 'Thus, the competence which is specifically envisaged as independent of any single mode bridges the gap between objectives and practice without merely reducing the objective to a recognizable "behaviour".' There are ten such competences: analysing; evaluating; exploring; expressing; interacting; narrating; retrieving; shaping; simulating; summarizing. Nine levels of achievements are to be distinguished within each, as in this example, the competence of Expressing:

Level 1 – To express and communicate feelings on a matter of personal concern.

Level 3 – To express and communicate convincingly feelings on matters of personal concern.

Level 5 – To express in some detail and communicate convincingly feelings and experience of personal and general concern.

Level 7 – To express feelings in detail and communicate sensitively the quality of experiences so that an effective and personal response is clearly evident.

Level 9 – To express feelings and the quality of experiences evocatively and sensitively without confusion and with insight and self-awareness.

I am indebted to my friend and colleague, Peter Doughty, for the suggestion that, had Jonathan Swift been aware of work like this, he would have added a sixth voyage to Part III of *Gulliver's Travels*, a voyage to the land of Criteria.

Some of the documents betray evidence of a process of education taking place, of education, that is, in the complexity of language and the concomitant difficulty of reducing measurement of achievement in language to some sort of linear progression. The enterprise resembles nothing so much as a gigantic Polo Mint, with at its core – where a linguistic model of language should have been installed – a yawning hole. This can be seen by reference to suggested criteria for establishing grade boundaries in written English which have come from two sources, the Working Party on National Criteria set up by the Secondary Examinations Council and the Northern Examining Association.

The SEC Draft proposals list the criteria for writing under three heads: Content; Organization and Structure; and the Use of Language. This tripartite division at least reveals an awareness of the fundamental problem in the assessment of writing, any assessment, graded or not. It is the problem of balancing regard for the content, i.e. *what* is being said, with regard for the way in which it is being said, i.e. the *how*. Nevertheless, the criteria set down under the Use of Language heading, despite a gesture towards a functional view of language in words like 'appropriate' and 'particular', rest essentially upon a 'flat-earth' view of language.

Use of Language

Candidates:

1 attempt to use language for particular effects
2 can use simple vocabulary appropriate to the task
3 can write in sentences
4 show evidence of an ability to
   (a) spell commonly used words correctly
   (b) apply common grammatical conventions as appropriate to the task
   (c) use some basic punctuation
5 attempt to use a style of writing appropriate to the adopted role and purpose.

In the first place, the items are confused in their levels of specificity and generality. The first requires evidence of an 'attempt to use language for particular effects'. What is meant here by 'particular', a notoriously empty word, one whose use in a context like this demands reference and definition? How is an assessor, lacking such guidance, expected to identify the attempts and judge their effectiveness? The following items will not give much help. 'Simple vocabulary'. In which model of language is vocabulary taken to be an independent level, suitable for assessment? What are to be the criteria of simplicity? Length? Frequency of usage? Does it refer to prepositions and conjunctions as well as nouns and verbs, adjectives and adverbs? Are they same category as the 'commonly used words, which, in item 4, candidates are expected to be able to spell correctly? Item 3 requires that candidates 'can write in sentences', item 4(c) that they can 'use some basic punctuation'. Is 3 referring to the grammatical construction of the sentence, irrespective of whether a full-stop has been placed at the end, or is it a demand for full-stops? If so, why include a demand for 'basic punctuation' separately? How, in any case, is 'basic' to be defined? Which uses of the full-stop and comma? And what can be meant by 4(b), 'apply common grammatical conventions as appropriate to the task'? If what the candidate has written is meaningful, which will have been assessed under Content, then he or she will have used 'common grammatical conventions', since meaning implies grammaticality. Or is there a hidden assumption, that some grammar is better than other grammar? Why not make the assumption explicit? However, if you do, you encounter difficulties of a different kind, as revealed in the draft proposals from the Northern Examining Association. These, like, indeed, those from the SEC Working Party, contain welcome elements. Among them are the emphasis given to talk as a means of promoting linguistic development, especially as part of a programme of integrated activities, and the opportunities for candidates to present course-work for the purposes of assessment. However, as with the SEC's Draft Criteria, the Northern proposals contain, at their heart, criteria for assessing writing that do not stand up to linguistic scrutiny. As we examine them, it is useful to bear in mind that, as we saw at the beginning of the chapter, the concept of graded assessment contains the promise that *objective* decisions can be made on the quality of the pupils' work, so that defined grade boundaries can be established to discriminate seven grades of performance.

A typical page of Northern proposals shows criteria for writing in what is called an 'open' situation. ('Closed' situations are, apparently, those in which 'subject matter, form, audience and purpose are largely given', and 'open' situations those in which 'such factors are largely determined by the writer'. The distinction, taken from the National Criteria, reflects a distinction between literary and non-literary language, and is difficult to sustain on linguistic grounds. Where is it supposed that writers in a so-called 'open' situation, especially apprentice writers, which is what pupils in school are, derive notions of appropriacy, form and style from?)

An immediate reservation comes with the first requirement under this head, 'ability . . . to communicate meaning at first reading.' Here we are in the presence of an idealized omniscient reader. Communication, in the world outside Grade Criteria, is always a two-way process. No meaning can be communicated unless the audience (listener or reader) takes part in the process, so that a meeting of minds may take place in the middle ground. To place *all* the onus on the writer is to enshrine a misconception about the nature of communication that places examinees at a permanent disadvantage.

The detailed criteria, like those from SEC, in the same search for apparent objectivity, abound with words and phrases of relativity, such as largely, generally, predominantly, usually. No hint is given of how the judgements might be applied in practice to actual pieces of writing, no mention made of any linguistic model from which they might derive meaning. But, then, it must be said, the naivety of the linguistic world into which we are invited to enter through these criteria is made sadly obvious.

As with the SEC criteria, candidates are expected to be able to use 'simple' vocabulary, spell 'commonly used' words, 'generally write in sentences', and 'usually apply common grammatical conventions'. They are open to the objections already noted. But they go further in their requirements for higher grades. Candidates must be able to 'match more complex ideas with more complex and varied sentences' and 'use . . . the more complex forms of punctuation.'

It is a kind of linguistic *Animal Farm*, where it is a case of 'two syllables good, four syllables better' or 'simple sentence good, complex sentence better'. Gordon Wells has warned against the assumptions underlying this kind of reasoning in his new book, *The Meaning Makers*.

24

. . . if two children differ in the frequency with which they are observed to use complex sentences, one using a wide variety of sentence types in several different contexts, is this the result of a real difference in ability or is it simply a difference in the sentence types that each chooses to use? Among educated adults, we would assume it was the latter. One might prefer William Faulkner to Ernest Hemingway, for example, but there would be little temptation to argue that Faulkner had greater linguistic ability simply on the grounds that his sentences were typically longer and more complex.

With young children, however, this is the assumption that is frequently made. Indeed, some writers have made the further assumption that more frequent use of complex structures is evidence of a more advanced level of intellectual functioning. As yet, however, this claim has not been systematically investigated and, until a causal connection has been clearly demonstrated, it would be wise to be more cautious.

Why, further, should it be supposed that four-syllable words are necessarily more difficult to spell than two-, or even one-syllable, words? Try 'yacht', for example. In her book *Period Piece*, Gwen Raverat says of her grandfather, Charles Darwin, that throughout the diary he kept during the voyage of the *Beagle*, he spelt yacht as 'yatch' and broad as 'broard'. By the time he came to publish it, he no doubt had his publisher's proof-reader to help him!

Using the criteria as given, in so far as that is possible, it would be interesting to see what sort of grade might be given for a piece of writing beginning like this:

'I was walking by the Thames. Half-past morning on an autumn day. Sun in a mist. Like an orange in a fried fish shop. All bright below. Low tide, dusty water and a crooked bar of straw, chicken-boxes, dirt and oil from mud to mud. Like a viper swimming in skim milk. The old serpent, symbol of nature and love.'[1]

Would the ability to write for a 'particular' effect outweigh the inability generally to write in sentences? If so, in what proportion?

25

Apart from the demonstrable fact that they rest upon inadequate linguistic foundations, proposals such as these suffer the further handicap that they start from the wrong end of the assessment process. This has been shown by the work of the Language Monitoring Team of the Assessment of Performance Unit, which, during a programme lasting five years, from 1979–83, looked at the work of nearly 50,000 Primary and 50,000 Secondary Pupils, aged 11 and 15 respectively. Work on the project began as far back as 1975, so that some ten years' experience has been accumulated. It is, therefore, quite remarkable that no formal approach to tap that experience was made by any of the groups working on graded assessment. Our education system has a notable facility for generating groups of people labouring behind their own fences. The output of the Team contains some valuable lessons for any kind of assessment, graded or otherwise.

In the first place, the work was based upon secure linguistic foundations. The functional perspective adopted led to two conclusions:

1 Since language is functional, pupils should be assessed over a range of tasks.
2 The model of assessment to be used for writing (and subsequently for oracy) should not only reflect the nature and function of language, but should be applied in practice by experienced teachers, well acquainted with what 11 and 15-year-olds are capable of achieving.

Two forms of assessment were applied to the scripts, impression and analytic. Analytic marking was based upon five criteria, which together might be expected to reveal in detail what the impression mark signified overall. The criteria were: Content; Organization; Appropriateness and style; Grammatical conventions; and Orthographic conventions. While it might be possible to focus on other features of writing, these five were regarded as being 'characteristic of all types of writing addressed to an audience'. Together, they enable a judgement to be made of the way in which a writer has deployed his/her linguistic resources in the fulfilment of a particular task. Answers can be given to the questions, What meaning has been made? How has it been communicated?

One of the most significant findings of the Monitoring Programme was that the performance of individual pupils varied according to the particular task they were attempting. A paragraph in the 1982 Primary Survey Report puts it like this:

> Ease or difficulty in writing, as measured by performance scores in analytic assessment, has been shown to have task-specific characteristics. This is the case for all but the extreme ends of the performance scale in the sense that, apart from the most able and the least able writers, for the majority of 11-year-olds, the ability to integrate the elements of the written language depends to some extent upon the nature of the task posed. In assessing children's writing analytically, we have noted the ways in which a number of 'basic' competencies required for the construction of a written text (control over propositional text, stylistic variations, grammatical and orthographic conventions, etc.) are handled with more or less success depending upon whether, for example, the task in question is a story, a letter or a plan. Our results suggest that the problems many 11-year-olds encounter with writing are specific to variations of written discourse rather than widespread across a whole range of tasks. . . .

It will be seen that this finding calls into question at once the validity of the GCE-type English Language exam, in which a candidate (and the task-specific characteristic holds good for the older pupils surveyed) is asked to pick a topic from a list and write upon it for forty-five minutes. (The list in a recent GCE paper included the topic, 'Chivalry, courtesy and romance are dead'. Are they?) Had the candidate picked a different topic from the one he or she decided to write on, the level of performance would have been different. Forty-five minutes' writing on a subject randomly selected from a list of six cannot be taken as evidence of some generalized writing ability. To obtain that, if put in such simplistic terms it can be said to exist at all, the kind of evidence yielded by a Mode 3 type course lasting four or five terms would be needed.

It also calls into question the approach to the devising of Graded Tests as revealed in the proposals so far published, where attempts have been made to devise criteria for grade boundaries without regard either to the task-specific nature of performance or the need for a linguistically adequate model of assessment. You cannot, in advance and in the abstract, set up a general category of writing, say 'Expressing', and then purport to erect grade boundaries by means of words like 'sensitively', or 'sensitively . . . in some detail', or 'evocatively and sensitively without confusion and with insight and self-awareness'. What distinguishes levels of performance in one task, let alone one category (whatever validity as a category it might have), will not become clear until after sufficient numbers of pupils have attempted the task, and their writing been carefully assessed. It follows from this that any task which it is proposed to ask pupils to undertake as part of any large-scale assessment scheme must first be piloted with a statistically adequate sample of pupils. The responses must then be assessed by experienced teachers trained in the use of a linguistically sophisticated model of assessment. *The criteria which distinguish levels of performance will then emerge from the writing*. If a judgement properly representative of a pupil's achievement is to be obtained, then this exercise will need to be repeated over a wide, functionally useful range of tasks.

The concept of basing a judgement on a range of tasks is, of course, that of Mode 3, as developed originally for CSE, then used in GCE, and now offered in GCSE. It also happens to coincide with one of the pedagogic implications of the Language Monitoring, one that reveals the dangers inherent in the Graded Test movement. As well as surveying the writing performance of pupils, the Team collected two other bodies of evidence. They produced questionnaires designed to elicit from pupils what they thought of themselves as writers and what they considered to be the features of good writing. They also collected all the written work done in school by some of the pupils taking part in the surveys at the same time as the surveys were taking place. In this way, they were able to form an idea of the range of writing experiences pupils were having in the course of normal school-work.

Comparison of pupils' performances with answers to the questionnaires suggested that one of the most powerful factors affecting achievement is perception of the nature of the task, and of what its fulfilment demands. Such perceptions, it is clear, derive in part from experience of doing similar tasks, in part from self-belief in the ability to tackle the task, and in part from beliefs about the characteristics of good writing. These beliefs are largely founded on what pupils have been told by their teachers. Pupils need, if they are to develop their capabilities as writers, sensitive and helpful responses to their writing. Many, in answer to questionnaires, revealed their belief that the hall-marks of good writing were 'spelling and punctuation' (seen as one category) and neatness. The origins of these beliefs are doubtless the comments written by teachers at the end of pieces of writing done in school, a practice which appears to reflect a touching faith, despite all the evidence to the contrary, that the writing of such comments will have a beneficial effect on a pupil's ability to write.

There is a real danger that teachers who already place an over-reliance on the efficacy of such comments will simply continue to make them within the context of a curriculum bounded by Graded Tests because they will assume, as the proponents of the scheme would have them believe, that the motivation provided by the scheme will be sufficient, of itself, to guarantee progress, and that, if it doesn't, then it is because some pupils cannot be taught to write well.

In a working paper published by the Secondary Examinations Council called 'Coursework Assessment in GCSE'[2] there is a reference (on page 4) to candidates who 'suffer out of all proportion across a whole range of examination subjects because of difficulty in understanding and explaining themselves in written English'. Thus is revealed a belief, at what must now be regarded as the highest level of educational thinking, that some pupils are ineducable in an area central to the whole learning process. I have argued in a previous book in this series, *Teaching*

Writing, that the fact that some pupils leave secondary schools able to write little letter than they did when they entered five years previously can largely be ascribed to the methods used which purport to improve handling of the writing system. This will be discussed further in the next chapter. Meanwhile, it should be noted that the Adult Literacy Project has shown how pupils of all ages from 18–86 can be taught to read and write, providing effective methods are used. There is no reason at all why it should be regarded as inevitable, as this pamphlet appears to do, that some pupils will pass through secondary school without overcoming their difficulties in 'understanding and expressing themselves in written English'.

But there is a grave danger that, if it becomes accepted by teachers that a scheme of graded assessment will itself provide all the motivation necessary for a pupil to overcome those difficulties, and if, because of the amount of time that will have to devoted to administering the scheme, they are denied the opportunity to think properly about their pupils' problems, then pupils in need will continue to be denied the effective help they deserve.

Moreover, as Gordon Wells points out in *The Meaning Makers*, there is a further danger, that of confusing achievement with progress. Measures of achievement, which is what Graded Assessment purports to be, are, he says,

> biased against slow developers who, by definition, achieve low scores relative to their age peers. However, it does not follow at all that because a child remains at the bottom of the class throughout a year or even several years that he or she has made less *progress* than the child who was consistently at the top of the same class. Low achievers in a class may thus be making just as much progress as high achievers. In a highly competitive society, however, this is often treated as less important than the fact that they are slow developers. Always coming off worse in age-related comparisons of achievement, they may easily come to be seen and to see themselves as intrinsically less well able to learn and, as a result, cease to make the progress of which they are capable.

It was, no doubt, considerations like this that led James Hemming, in a letter to the *Guardian*, to describe an examination system which 'still retains the graded hierarchy of assessment' as being 'destructive of the poor scholar's self-respect'.

The entry against the word 'curriculum' in my *Smaller Latin Dictionary* gives, as its meaning, 'a running, course. . . . Esp a race, raceground, racecourse.' Graded assesement, as so far proposed, will succeed only in adding to the race a succession of hurdles, placed at arbitrary intervals. Perhaps the National Criteria should be renamed the Grand National Criteria, with the first two words constituting one lexical item.

3 'Needs urgent attention'

The traditional way of responding to the writing that pupils do in the course of their English lessons in school, or their English homework, is the process known as marking, a word which reveals the whole point of the operation. This requires the teacher to proof-read what the pupil has written, and put a mark and a comment at the end. It entails, on the part of the teacher, a huge investment of time, time which – if it is supposed to bring about improvement in performance – is largely wasted. Nevertheless, it is widely regarded as an essential part of the duties of those teachers whose subject requires the setting of writing tasks.

The following are typical of comments to be found at the end of written work:

Some very good descriptive words and phrases but you are not writing in correct sentences
Grammar weak in places
Very many mistakes here – study them carefully
Too many errors for a pass grade
There are many more mistakes in this than I have been able to indicate
Sentence-structure and punctuation weak
Sentence-structure needs urgent attention

The teacher who had written these comments was a gifted teacher – of English Literature. Therein lies the explanation of how it comes about that committed teachers who care about their pupils' welfare can continue to put their faith in teaching methods (and the practice of marking *is* – or purports to be – a teaching method) that patently do not work. The comments quoted occurred in the exercise book of a boy in the fifth form of a comprehensive school. He had thus been in the school for four and a half years. GCE was a term away. If, as the teacher believed, the boy's sentence-structure needed 'urgent attention', why then (assuming that he was not suffering from a sudden breakdown in sentence-structure) had it not been given earlier in his school career? From whom, and how, was he supposed to be receiving this attention? There was no evidence in his book of any work designed to remedy his defect. What then is the writing of the comment supposed to achieve? What was meant by the earlier comment, 'You are not writing in correct sentences'? That the ends of sentences were not being signalled by full-stops, or that full-stops were being placed at the end of incomplete grammatical structures? Or both, as suggested by the comment, 'Sentence-structure *and* punctuation weak.' How was the boy supposed to know? In one comment, he is enjoined to study his mistakes carefully, but what is the point of that? It is at least arguable that, if you understand the nature of the mistake you are making, you won't make it in the first place, and also that you will need both explanation and help if you are to avoid making it in future. Self-help is not enough.

The remarks made by the teacher in this case are representative of those traditionally made in the course of marking. They are the outward and visible signs of an approach to the teaching of English that has dominated the educational scene for over a hundred years, and has been responsible for generations of pupils emerging from what Mr Polly called 'the valley of the shadow of education' able to write much less well than they could. The reason why this is allowed to happen is simple. It is that most teachers, whether of English or any other subject, are not given a linguistic perspective on language during their training. The *Bullock Report* noted this fact, and called for a 'substantial course on language in education' to be included in the initial training of every primary and secondary school teacher. That goal is still far from being achieved.

It is very rare for courses leading to degrees in Eng. Lit., whether in Universities or Polytechnics, to contain any, let alone any 'substantial', element concerned with language, linguistically perspectived. During my time as an English Inspector with the ILEA, I interviewed annually, at Easter, numbers of students at the end of their courses seeking teaching appointments. Very few had done anything significant on language during their training, either in the 'professional' part or the 'educational'. That one has to use the terms points to a disabling weakness in the system by which teachers are prepared to take their places in the classroom, because language is frequently allowed to slip through the middle. Learning may be treated from a Piagetian, cognitive development, perspective, but rarely from a linguistic one. The result is that many teachers, of English, as well as other subjects, enter upon their careers with their folk-linguistic notions, their flat-earth view, unimpaired.

In this sort of situation, it is very easy for the syndrome already noted to become established:

Some pupils have difficulty with spelling and punctuation
They do not respond to traditional methods of 'teaching'
Therefore they are ineducable.

The tragedy is that even those teachers who are unwilling to accept this proposition find it impossible to break out because they do not have an intellectual framework which would permit them to approach the problem from a different angle. Moreover, they are liable to discover, if they do try to break out, that they have the whole world, or what seems like the whole world, against them. There are English syllabuses which, like many of the pronouncements emanating from the DES, are very glib at setting out aims and objectives, but are very reticent at suggesting how these might be achieved. There are colleagues, senior colleagues, colleagues in other departments, who believe that, because some pupils continue to have difficulties with spelling and punctuation, you are not doing anything about it, or do not care about it, when you are, in fact, religiously doing about it what most people have always done, and with the same

35

notable lack of success. The beliefs held, say, by senior colleagues, are also shared by parents (some, anyway) and commentators. This last category includes not only journalists but also, revealingly, many in Higher Education, like the authors of the Black Papers which, with their characteristic combination of political bias and intellectual poverty in the late sixties and early seventies, showed yet again that the possession of high positions in Eng. Lit. is no guarantee of a linguistic knowledge of language, or of how this might be invested in effective teaching.

The position of the course-book in all this is very instructive. As I argued in *Teaching Writing*, whatever the changes in format and presentation, and the inclusion of new ideas, such as group discussion, many retain, at their core, exercises purporting to assist pupils in difficulty with spelling and punctuation. In *Teaching Writing* I poked fun at the practice of having pupils rewrite sentences, in the singular or plural as appropriate, like 'I sent her a ripe strawberry', 'Daily she sees the larch in the forest' or 'Daisies shed their petals'. I was recently sent, for comment, a manuscript in which there were exercises containing sentences such as

The dwarf gave the lady a kiss.
The man riding the white stallion is a bachelor.
The waiter served his father.

The first was among those to be rewritten in the plural, the other two to be rewritten in the feminine. They are, perhaps, extreme examples of the kind of exercise in which publishers, through course-books, invite teachers to put their faith.

That publishers themselves continue to have faith is apparent from the blurbs in their catalogues. So, too, is underlying linguistic confusion.

. . . . provides exercises to help less able students improve their language skills. . . . written for those students who have a high motivation for passing examinations, yet whose language is extremely limited, possibly because they read little outside school or college. It aims to expand these students' existing knowledge of the written form by widening their vocabulary and improving their style, thus facilitating the fluent expression of ideas.

Those 'whose language is extremely limited' are pupils who speak English as their native tongue, and are within sight of O level or CSE. At least, the book's place in the catalogue suggests this. There is the attempt to connect 'extremely limited' language (whatever that might mean) with (possibly) too little reading, followed by the claim that 'existing knowledge of the written form' may be expanded by 'widening their vocabulary and improving their style', both to be achieved through exercises. None of this betrays any real understanding of language as a human attribute, and its deployment in speech, in reading and writing. But if, despite this lack, the book actually achieved for the pupil what it claims, why is there need for other books in the same catalogue for which similar claims are made?

> contains guidance and many exercises covering the skills of punctuation, spelling, vocabulary, use of capitals, recognition of homophones, line-end divisions and so on. Written for 11–14 year olds of average and above average ability, this book contains passages with exercises and assignments to teach pupils the basic patterns of punctuation and can be used either as a course, or to provide practice in specific aspects of punctuation which may give difficulty.

The linguistic confusion is announced at once, in the list of so-called 'skills', where vocabulary is included, as a skill, on the same level as punctuation, which is separated from use of capitals by two items, and spelling, which has 'recognition of homophones' singled out as a sub-category, but again separated by two items. There follows a reference to 'basic patterns of punctuation'. What does this mean? Pairs of commas round parts of sentences? In any case, if the book can successfully teach them, why does it also offer to deal with 'specific aspects of punctuation which may give difficulty'? There is, as everybody knows, one specific aspect that does cause difficulty. It is the use

37

of the full-stop to mark the end of a sentence, a problem which will be discussed towards the end of the chapter.

Faith in definitions as an aid to learning, and in the use of tests, is also declared.

> . . . provides a series of simple, enjoyable exercises to help them understand grammatical terms. Definitions are provided, but explanations are kept as simple as possible. . . .
>
> Tests at the beginning and throughout the book mean that students' ability can be assessed before embarking on the scheme and their progress measured during the course. . . . primarily intended for 11–16 year olds, but would be suitable for any competent reader who needs to remedy a spelling problem.

Why, if we are considering writing, do we need tests to tell us what our pupils are achieving? Can this not be seen from the writing that they are, presumably, doing regularly as part of their course? The reference to 'ability' and later to 'progress' suggests some confusion between 'ability' and 'performance', but progress can, and can only, be deduced from performance of writing tasks, not in the doing of decontextualized tests. There is a further confusion in that particular blurb, evidenced in the reference to 'any competent *reader* who needs to remedy a *spelling* problem'. It is writers who need to remedy spelling problems.

The catalogue from which these examples have been taken not only reveals the full pretension of the course-book lobby, but also (no doubt inadvertently) gives the game away.

For a 'Graded English Course' (note how quickly fashionable words like 'Graded' are taken on board) suitable for pupils between the ages of 12 and 16 the following claim is made:

> This English course is designed to teach basic skills to non-examination classes in a lively modern format. It provides practice in three basic areas: the skills associated with the written and spoken aspects of English; certain everyday tasks which children encounter on leaving school; and, to make a break from more formal exercises, some informal activities.

The books of which the course is composed are said either to 'deal with the mechanics of English' (with 'leisure breaks' to refresh and stimulate the pupil, which will clearly be needed) or to 'provide intensive practice in essential skills'. The model of language which enables author and publisher to use words like 'mechanics' and 'practice' in respect of 'spoken aspects of English' with which pupils have been acquainted for almost twelve years before encountering these books is not one which linguists would readily recognize.

However, the blurb which finally gives the game away is that which says of a particular book,

> . . . can be used consecutively or as a resource for teachers to give pupils who persistently make the same mistake.

Persistently make the same mistake? What has happened to the certainty with which the benefits of other books were extolled, to the exercises which promised to *cover* the skills of this or that, the practice which would extend this aptitude or expand that knowledge? How does it come about that, faced with all this help, pupils can possibly persist in making the same mistakes?

It comes about, and this should hardly need repeating, because the word games which the use of these books encourages do not feed productively into the ability to use language, whether in speech or writing, or for the purposes of reading, in real situations, and we will, for the moment, regard demands made in the classroom as 'real'. The games rarely go to the heart of the matter. As with quack doctors of old, both diagnosis and remedy are faulty, and for the same reason. The lack of a scientific model on which to base either. Take one last blurb from the unhappy catalogue which has been the source of quotation:

> . . . to help pupils to write sentences. It has been written for those who may be capable of interesting creative writing but all too frequently cannot punctuate it because they do not understand the patterns of the English sentence.

If the pupils for whom this book claims to have been written are 'capable of interesting creative writing', then they are capable of writing in grammatical structures, and of linking them together in some sort of narrative. Meaning implies grammaticality. To the making and conveying of meaning grammatical structures are essential. And to any sort of narrative the use of words and phrases to link grammatical structures together (to give the writing *cohesion*) is necessary. If they are 'capable of interesting creative writing' then they are capable of writing grammatically and linking it together.

What they may not always be doing is marking sentences with full-stops, despite all the exercises they may have done, and all the notes they may have copied from the blackboard – lists which often include, beside all possible uses of the full-stop, eight uses of the comma, colons, semi-colons, apostrophes and dashes. This is not what is required by a pupil who is unsure of the primary use of the full-stop: that of marking the end of a sentence. What is required is an approach based upon existing knowledge of language, that is, the spoken language. (See Appendix.)

Spoken language is what nearly everybody learns, and learns to experience, from birth. The exceptions are those born with less than normal brains, or with a handicap such as deafness that interferes with what is otherwise a natural process. From hearing it around them, children gradually develop their own language. The usual environment for this is the family. The sounds of the language are learnt, the uses to which it is put are experienced. Children teach themselves (quite literally) to understand and use language, to express emotions, to ask and answer questions, to give, and obey, orders, and so on. They are able to do this because the child's brain is capable of abstracting from the sounds of language heard all around the rules which govern its use, and then to translate those rules back into language that its owner can use for her or himself. The three-year-old who says, after a drink, 'Me needed that' has already taught himself to make the past tense of 'need', and to use the word 'that' as a pronoun to refer to the action in question. He has also taught himself a rule for the use of the personal pronoun referring to himself, namely that you use the word 'me', as indeed you do in structures like, 'Give me that' or 'Pass that to me'. In time he will teach himself the further rule that will enable him to say. 'I needed that.' It is possible to say that the use of 'me' in 'Me needed that' is wrong. It is much more sensible to regard it (and there is adequate evidence for this) as a stage in normal language development. The one is a flat-earth view, the other, rather more heliocentric.

Young children come to understand, intuitively, from their experience of what other people are saying, and how, and their own developing ability to make themselves understood, what constitutes a meaningful 'chunk' of language, something that may be made meaningful by its combination of sounds, words, stress and intonation, sometimes supported by gestures and other para-linguistic features. By the time they enter school at, usually, the age of five, they have a good working knowledge of language, and some intuitive understanding of what makes it work. They then have to learn to read and write.

This means, in effect, deploying the language that they have acquired as a system of sounds through the process of primary language acquisition in the business of mastering a language system operating in a visual medium through symbols on paper. The relationship between the two systems, speech and writing, is complex. It is not the simple one-to-one relationship between a sound and a visual system that is sometimes supposed, with the business of writing amounting to little more than putting on paper the 'sentences' in which we speak. Nobody, in fact, talks spontaneously in 'sentences'. The speech of normal exchanges between people consists typically of a succession of linguistic structures, single words sometimes, which carry meaning because they occur in a shared context in which speaker and listener (or listeners) can supply, or, if necessary, ask for, the requisite clues. Formal speeches, which are liable to be couched in sentences, occur in contexts which preclude this kind of interchange. In writing, too, the author has to create a context in which the meaning he or she is trying to convey becomes accessible to readers.

Learning to write entails, therefore, learning to write in

sentences, because that is the conventional way of conveying meaning in writing. It does seem that some people learn to do this almost as naturally as they learn to speak, while others do not. And many of those, given the traditional and ineffective ways of 'helping' them, never overcome the difficulty. Despite this, and despite the work of the Adult Literacy Project and of others who approach the problem from a linguistic perspective, barren practices continue to be recommended in course-books.

These course-books remain as a sort of sub-culture, impervious to outside influence, transmitting a tradition of ineffective teaching from generation to generation. It is not as if teaching materials based upon a proper linguistic foundation were not being produced, or as if developments like Mode 3, which call for new ways of approaching old tasks, were not proving popular. Yet there persists, at the heart of the teaching of English, a core of practices which have no pedagogic value. Only those with a flat-earth perspective could suppose that they had. They go back, in memory, to their own school-days, supposing that their own ability to handle written language owes something to the exercises they did, knowing, too, that the doing of exercises sometimes leads to quiet, if not productive, activity in the class-room. Course-books lend their spurious authority, and so the cycle is repeated. That it should be broken, that means be found of injecting into the training of teachers a satisfactory intellectual model of language, is the matter that, above all else, 'needs urgent attention.'

Before it can be discussed further, however, it is necessary to answer the question, 'What is it, exactly, that you are saying teachers need to know about language?' It is the subject of the next chapter.

4 What do teachers need to know about language?

Despite the way in which linguists have, over the last four decades, added immeasurably to our knowledge of language, its structure, and the way it works, no full and satisfactory answer to the question at the head of the chapter has yet been incorporated into teacher training. As HMI surveys have confirmed, the language components in teacher training courses remain, on the whole, scrappy and inadequate. Since pupils' success in school depends crucially on their ability to develop their linguistic resources in order to meet the demands being made upon them, the lack of an adequate linguistic background in their teachers will have serious consequences, especially for those pupils in most need of help and support.

It was appreciation of this that led group of English teachers in the ILEA, who came together in 1980 to try to answer the question, to list as the first two of their six points the following:

1 Children acquire and develop the ability to talk, naturally, as a system of communication, through their own direct experience of language as they grow up. At the same time, language is social, exists already in the society into which children are born, and offers its users both choice and constraints.

2 Meaning is embodied in language. Sophisticated communication, which is an essential part of human life, is only possible between people who share the same language.

Human beings are genetically programmed to acquire language. They are born with language-learning brains, except in a tiny minority of cases where a defect prevents natural

43

development. This means that, except in those few cases, all that is necessary for language to develop is that the child should grow up in an environment in which language is being used. That is, in any normal environment with a group of other human beings. We are now more aware of the speed at which early language development takes place, and therefore are better able to appreciate the child's staggering achievement in laying the foundations of his or her mastery of the complex phenomenon we call language by the age of two.

The language that children learn has a twin aspect. It is an individual possession, it is uniquely theirs, and yet it is social, existing as it does to enable people to communicate with each other. The point, the essence, of language is to communicate, to make meaning. The language system, or systems, that people possess constitute a resource for making meaning. (A parenthesis is necessary as a reminder that many people grow up with more than one language, and are bi-, even tri-, lingual.) They draw upon this resource to meet the demands of everyday living. Language has developed as it has in order to satisfy those demands. This is what has given it its functional character, and it is this approach to the study of language that constitutes a functional perspective.

For children between the ages of 5 and 16 in the United Kingdom 'everyday living' includes going to school. Schools, especially Comprehensive Schools, bring together children from different communities, speaking not only different forms of a common language, English, as their mother-tongue, but, in a city like London, some 140 other languages as their first language.

The third point made by the ILEA teachers, with English specifically in mind, states:

3   All dialects are linguistically equal. If some dialects of English are more highly regarded than others, this reflects a socially constructed hierarchy. Such hierarchies have developed an aura of naturalness round their particular linguistic forms, so that deviations from them are seen as unnatural, incorrect, inferior.

The reference to a 'socially constructed hierarchy' reflects the status that has been traditionally accorded to the dialect known as Standard English, with its implication that other dialects are somehow inferior. This has already been discussed in the Introduction as a product of the class-structure. There is here a paradox worth noting. It is that, very often, those who extol the virtues of family life as a basis for social order do not scruple to denigrate that most important family possession, its language, if it does not happen to fit into a particular category. Any such tendency, on the part of a teacher, will succeed in erecting a barrier around children whose mother-dialect puts them into an 'inferior' category, hindering their ability to communicate and denying them access to educational opportunities. If teachers are not to connive at the erection of such artificial barriers, their intellectual equipment must include a thorough understanding of concepts like accent, dialect and variety.

Language exists in two forms, as speech and as writing. It used to be thought (by some it still is, it seems) that writing was the superior form of language, with speech being somehow a debased form. (The word 'grammar', to be discussed in the next section, derives, in fact, from a Greek word meaning 'to write'.) What was never more than a myth has now been exploded, at least as far as the world of linguistic scholarship is concerned: speech and writing are seen as being equally complex, but in different ways. The development of tape-recorders in the last three and a half decades has permitted a more detailed exploration of the nature of speech, as well as contributing to enhanced understanding of language-learning in infancy and of the part that spoken language plays in human life from the beginning. Nevertheless, reading and writing play a crucial part in education, and this is reflected in the next point.

4 Spoken language has primacy over written language. Talk came before writing in the development of language, while the ability to talk develops before the ability to write in the lives of individuals. Talk is immensely important to

learning. Literacy, however, is a sign of education in our society, and is the means through which much highly valued knowledge is transmitted and, indeed, constructed.

Something has already been said, in Chapter 3 , of the difficulties that some children experience when learning to write, and of the demands that these difficulties make (or should make) on their teachers. As the next point insists, it is important for teachers to understand that:

5 The relationship of spoken to written language is complex. It is important to know something of the function of writing in representing speech visually; of differences between the two modes; and of the features which are specific to writing.

This formulation refrains from going into detail, contenting itself with an insistence, in general terms, on the importance of knowing something about the complex relationship between speech and writing. It does not ask how much knowledge about the structure of language is required *before* the relationship between speech and writing can be properly understood. Among the subsidiary questions in this area is that of 'grammar', which, usually understood as being synonymous with parts of speech, furnished the starting-point of this book.

Misunderstandings about grammar, what it is, and the part that knowledge of grammar plays in language development, are fundamental to the flat-earth perspective. 'Latin grammar is the only grammar' declared a speaker at a school's Speech day, as if the way in which a long-dead language was traditionally described had some special properties. More recently, a columnist in *The Times* wrote 'English doesn't have any grammar.' How he could suppose that English, or any other language, could function without a describable structure is difficult to see, unless it is the case that being a Classical Scholar had, in effect, furnished him with an intellectual strait-jacket from which no escape was possible.

It is not only that the study of Greek and Latin has traditionally required the study of their grammars as a bodies of knowledge which require to be learnt, but also that this study adopts a different perspective from a contemporary functional approach. What might be termed the 'Greek' view of grammar starts from the *forms* of words and sentences (which is what, in folk-linguistic terms, language is seen to consist of) and asks what the forms *mean*. By contrast, a functional approach starts from the other end, by acknowledging that the function of language is to make meaning, and by asking, 'How do linguistic forms achieve this?'

It is more important to see to it that intending teachers know what grammar is, than it is to ask the question, 'How much grammar do teachers of English need to know?' It is an observable fact that infants teach themselves their mother-tongue (or tongues) without any explicit grammar teaching. (How many parents would be equipped to do that?) It has already been argued, to a wearisome degree, that there is no necessary correlation between teaching grammar (for example, if you will, parts of speech) to pupils, and their progress as readers and writers. But it will be helpful for teachers who want to understand what may be happening in a pupil's writing, or who may want to discuss aspects of writing, to be able sometimes to refer explicity to the structure of the writing. They will need therefore, to be able to call upon a description of the language, a grammar.

There are many ways of describing how a language works, any language – witness the different descriptions offered by contemporary linguists like Chomsky and Halliday. Their descriptions reflect the perspective from which they approached the task of observing, and then describing, how linguistic forms convey the meaning they do. However, modern linguistic studies share a body of technical terms in which to talk about language, and beliefs about its basic structure.

In the last chapter, the predicament of those who do not seem able to learn how to use a full-stop in English was discussed, together with the unhelpful nature of the remedial action that teachers often resort to. A better perception of the way in which words, word groups, phrases, and clauses work together to make meaningful sentences in written English would clearly be helpful to teachers and, through them, their pupils. It is not enough to think simply in terms of words (vocabulary) and sentences, as in the crude linguistic models underlying the draft grade criteria. As M.A.K. Halliday points out in *An Introduction to Functional Grammar*, 'Describing a sentence as a construction of words is rather like describing a house as a construction of bricks, without recognizing the walls and the rooms as intermediate structural units.'[1] Teachers need a more sophisticated understanding than that, if they are to engage in meaningful dialogue with pupils.

In this sort of dialogue, it is not so much a matter of teaching *explicitly* about language, but of enabling pupils to make explicit for themselves the knowledge of language, and of how it works, that, as language-users, they already possess. As anyone who has watched an Infants class working with *Breakthrough to Literacy*[2] can testify, young children do not need to be *taught* grammar in order to learn to read and write. Using the Sentence Maker, they invest their existing, implicit, knowledge of the rules of combination (sounds into words, words into meaningful structures) in order to make visible meaning. This is not to argue, of course, that there is no requirement on the teacher's part to intervene in the learning process, to explain, discuss problems, suggest strategies.

But the needs are the pupils' needs. To teach Parts of Speech, as demanded by English 5–16, without relating them to the needs of the pupils, is ultimately to foist on children an arbitrary body of knowledge which has no relevance to their needs, and plays no part in the learning process. It is curious that the document in question adopts, on the whole, a functional approach to language, with the sections on Parts of Speech, deriving as they do from a quite different intellectual (if that is the appropriate word) tradition, standing out as an alien presence added as an afterthought.

Perhaps this compelling urge on the part of those concerned with the teaching of English, whether as teachers, writers or

48

inspectors, to teach *something*, however intellectually suspect, stems from a belief that teachers of so-called academic subjects are in the business of passing on knowledge, and that, if you aren't doing it, your status as a teacher is liable to be called into question. The truth is rather that, so far as work in English Language is concerned (for native speakers), pupils bring with them what they need to know. The teacher's role is to help them, to show them, how to make best use of it.

There is an analogy here with the job of PE teachers, whose task is to develop the use of the body. The anatomy they learn in the course of their training is not necessarily for passing on to pupils. It is to enable them to understand better what they are doing in the gym or on the playing-fields to promote the physical development of their pupils.

It was considerations like this that led the ILEA teachers to the formulation of their last proposal:

6 Teachers should have some understanding of the nature and purposes of language, and its relationship to society, if pupils are to be helped to develop their full and active potential as users of language. That potential, whether in speech or in writing, is developed more by experience than by correction.

The classroom has been described (by M.A.K. Halliday) as a 'socio-linguistic context', a phrase which recognizes pupils as language-users, not as fodder for exercises. Halliday also talks about 'classroom linguistics', concerned specifically with the nature of the demands made upon pupils' language, with the constraints operating upon their responses, and with how knowledge of language, as discussed in this chapter, would assist teachers as they help pupils overcome those restraints. 'Classroom Linguistics' should be a compulsory element, with adequate time devoted to it, in the training of every teacher, no matter his or her destination in the education service. We might then begin to realize the ambition of Primary Recommendation 15 of the *Bullock Report*:

15 A substantial course on language in education (including reading) should be part of every primary and secondary school teacher's initial training, whatever the teacher's subject or the age of the children with whom he or she will be working.

5 'Delivering the curriculum'

In a recent DES Green Paper, *Parental Influence at School*, there occurs this statement:

'A school's task is to equip pupils for adult life by developing all their qualities and talents. It does this by delivering the curriculum during and outside the time-tabled periods of instruction.'

It is a breathtakingly simplistic assertion, which suggests that 'delivering the curriculum' is a process rather like tipping a sack of coals into an empty bunker. Enough has been said, in the preceding chapters, about the linguistic foundations of learning to demonstrate that it is a much more complex process than that. One who recognized this was the late Derek Morrell, the possessor of one of the keenest minds to have been brought to bear on educational problems since the war. In a lecture given in 1968, the year before he died, he addressed himself to the nature of the learning process.[1]

To understand what is really going on in school, we have to come to grips with extremely complex, constantly changing and immensely particular systems of personal interaction, involving complex relationships between the experience, language and values which the pupils bring into school from their homes and neighbourhoods, and those which are imported by the teacher.

In a nutshell, if there is positive reciprocity of feeling and aspiration as between the teachers and the taught, satisfying to both, there is a describable curricular reality: the teachers are contributing to the learning which is taking place, they are helping to create new realities. But if there is no such reciprocity, if there is a total absence of mutual emotional satisfaction, the curriculum remains simply an idea in the minds of the teachers: it lacks reality, even though the teachers teach and the children go through the motions of scholastic activity.

He went on to argue that

> the curriculum – if it exists at all – is a structure erected on a base of reciprocal personal relationships . . . in curriculum we are concerned with human beings whose feelings and aspirations are far more real and immediately important to them than the cognitive development which is the educators' main stock-in-trade.

He warned against one possible implication of what he was saying:

> I am emphatically not saying that all should be sweetness and light, that permissiveness should reign supreme, that it does not matter what the children learn, or that cognitive development is of secondary importance. On the contrary, it matters very much what the children learn, and cognitive development is of primary importance.

He then restated his central thesis.

> *My point is rather that it is a waste of time to fuss about what we think the children should learn if we do not understand how to organize a system of pupil–teacher relationships which is productive of our intended learnings.*

There is no question here of simply 'delivering the curriculum'. Instead, there is a realistic view of the learning process which has been arrived at by asking first of all the question, 'What do children bring with them to the learning situation?' His answer is, 'experience, language and values', all derived from the environment in which the individual child has grown up. Of these, language is the most significant, since it not only represents the primary resource for learning, but is also the primary means by which that experience has taken on some some definitive lasting form, and the primary means by which the values have been transmitted and kept up.

After leaving the Schools Council, Derek Morrell moved to the Home Office, to work with the Children's Development Group. It was through that link that the trials of the *Language in Use* materials (developed by a Schools Council Project) included Approved Schools, as they were then called, where the value of the materials in helping pupils to invest their own language in the learning process was quickly recognized. (I remember one teacher, reporting on the way in which a *Language in Use* unit had been used to promote discussion in class, saying, 'It was as if those kids were being listened to for the first time in their lives.') Thus, when he spoke of 'experience, language and values', Derek Morrell was speaking from direct knowledge and experience of the part that language plays in learning. He was also, quite clearly, emphasizing the responsibility of the teacher for organizing learning situations that were productive of learning.

One of the educational success stories of the last ten years has been the Adult Literacy Project, started by the BBC in the mid seventies. It has catered for people of all ages from 16 to 86, thereby proving that, whatever may be asserted to the contrary, throughout this century there have always been those who have come through the school system of the time with their ability to read and write insufficiently established to last into adulthood.

The reasons for the success of the Project do not consist wholly of the fact that pupil and tutor are, in the early stages, in a one-to-one relationship, important as that is. They have more to do with the fact that tutors are trained to start where the student is, and to teach for success. Thus, they take great care to find out what the students' interests are, and what, if anything, they can read and write already, before a programme is planned. They try to ensure that, by the end of every session, students can do something, and acknowledge that they can do something, that they couldn't do at the beginning. If after two or three weeks it becomes obvious that the planned programme is not producing sufficiently desirable results, then it is scrapped and another one substituted. You cannot, as a tutor in a one-to-one situation with a student, go on meeting week after week if the student is palpably making no progress. The tutor has not only to assume responsibility for the student's learning; his or her status as a tutor is invested in it. This is in contrast to the situation in schools, where the teacher's status seems to be bound up with his or her role as a purveyor of knowledge. If a pupil does not succeed in acquiring this knowledge, the blame is seen to lie with the pupil rather than with the teacher.

Professor Brian Simon has argued, in 'Why No Pedagogy in England?',[2] that there was a time when it was believed that 'failure to develop positive attitudes, skills and abilities in the child may be a product of the teacher's own behaviour, or lack of skills, knowledge and method. Later interpretations of failure as the inevitable function of innate *disabilities in the child*, e.g. lack of intelligence, do not figure.'

There is a certain irony in the fact that the time referred to is the last decade of the nineteenth century, which saw the introduction of elementary education, and that the 'later interpretations of failure' grew alongside the development of secondary education in this century. Restricted access to secondary schools meant that some form (or forms) of selection were needed, and the concept of 'innate intelligence', largely as enunciated by Cyril Burt, proved to be a useful tool. Burt, whose evidence has been shown to have been based on fraudulent data, claimed that 'intelligence' could be measured 'with accuracy and ease'. This notion, which gained wide currency, had the lamentable effect of persuading generations of teachers that their pupils could be divided into two categories: those who were educable, and those who were not. It was a categorization that fitted very well with the concept of the teacher as the transmitter of knowledge. Some could 'receive' it, others could not.

More than an echo of this kind of argument can be heard in statements like, 'Mechanical accuracy in the writing of English, for example, will come or will not come, with maturity, and there is very little that teacher or text-book can do about it.' (Denys Thompson, in his Introduction to Alec Clegg's *The*

54

Excitement of Writing.[3]) We are now in a position to know, to believe, differently, but until teachers are intellectually equipped, through their training, to think through the fallacy for themselves, and change their methods, pupils will continue to remain in a state of 'needing urgent attention' but not getting it.

It is not, of course, only teachers who have been in the grip of this wrong-headed view of educability. It has been shared by politicians and administrators, who between them have responsibility for running the system; by those who have assumed responsibility for examining the products of the system; and by those who set themselves up to comment on matters educational.

If this were not the case, then we would not have developed, during the last twenty years or so, an educational system of comprehensive schools, based upon the notion of equal opportunities for all, within which has continued to operate a scheme of public examinations intended for a system of education based upon selection at 11-plus. That system was, in a brutal sense, designed to educate for failure.

Between 20 and 25 per cent (according to which part of the country you lived in) of pupils from primary schools were selected, by means of the 11-plus, to go on to Grammar Schools. Of these, some 40 per cent would emerge, after five years, as failures, since the O-Level pass rate was set at about 60 per cent. Only that 60 per cent, of the 20-odd per cent who entered Grammar School, could be said to have achieved any acknowledged success in the system. O-Level, the instrument of the system, continued in Comprehensive Schools, side by side with CSE, the examination system devised for Secondary Modern Schools at the insistence of teachers who believed that their pupils should have something tangible to show for their five years of secondary schooling. Now, belatedly, the introduction of GCSE signifies the acceptance of a need for a common system to serve Comprehensive Schools. It is, however, a tragedy of large proportions that the idea of a common exam should have become linked to the notion of graded assessment, which, in the form in which it seems to be developing, bids fair to institutionalize the message of failure as brutally, if more subtly, than the dual system it replaces.

'Delivering the curriculum' is a phrase that slips easily off the pens of those charged, at whatever level, with running an educational system. It connotes a system whereby a collection of packages of knowledge is delivered to recipients sitting meekly at desks, accepting what is deemed to be good for them. It supposes that the setting of aims and objectives will, of itself, be enough to ensure that they are achieved. It represents a naive view of education, and of learning.

Some years ago, on a holiday in France, I visited a vigneron in Beaune, to whom I had been given a letter of introduction. Before allowing us, with his assistant, to see the cellars, he talked to us about the making of wine. 'We try,' he said, 'to provide the conditions under which the wine can educate itself.' I remember thinking at the time that, if we were half as successful with our pupils as he was with his Beaujolais, we would have cause to congratulate ourselves.

6 Delivering the goods

Language in Use, as I see it, is the opening up of an important area of human potential. I use the ambiguous expression 'opening up' deliberately, to mean both making this potential available and bringing it to the light of day. *Language in Use* is a charted voyage of conquest and discovery, in which the pupil can explore, in terms of his own experience, the potential which lies at the heart of his understanding of that experience (and therefore of all his learning), namely, his mastery of language. The mastery of language, it should be insisted, is not simply the ability to say what one means; rather, it is the ability to mean. Each one of us has this ability, and lives by it; but we do not always become aware of it or realize fully the breadth and depth of its possibilities.

M.A.K. Halliday, Foreword to *Language in Use*[1]

It is now nearly fifteen years since *Language in Use* saw the light of day. Its intellectual, its linguistic, base has not been seriously challenged during that time, but some of the research and developments in classroom practice that have taken place in the meantime would now lead us to further conclusions. The intention of this chapter is to bring together some of the arguments, ideas and insights that have been expressed in earlier chapters, and ask what might be the implications for the English curriculum, both content and process: what it contains, and how it is taught. *The latter is more important than the former*.

First of all, there is the idea, given expression in Professor Halliday's Foreword, that language is, for the individual, both a resource and a potential. It is a genetico-social inheritance, transmitted by a particular context of family and community, at a particular place, in a particular milieu, at a given point in time. This inheritance will constitute, for any individual, the foundation of learning within, and beyond, the educational system. *The importance of understanding this cannot be exaggerated.*

The child's early experience of language, as used in the environment into which he or she is born, is greatly significant. This embraces not only the question of which language, or which variety of which language (e.g. English, or Gujerati, or Turkish, or one of the 140-odd other languages currently spoken as first languages by children in London schools), but also the question of the uses to which language is put in the business of living. What do those who share the environment with the child use language for? Asking questions, giving answers? Discussing? Explaining? Exploring? Story-telling? Reading? Writing? Are adults seen doing either of the last two linguistic activities? Do children grow up knowing, understanding, that language can be used for such activities, and why? It is in early experiences at this level that intuitive understanding of the functional nature of language, and of its possibilities, develops – or not, as the case may be. If, for example, parents do not bother to *explain* to children, either because they cannot be bothered or because they mistakenly believe that there is no point until children can respond properly, then children may grow up unaware of what is possible in language, and without experience of using the relevant linguistic structures. Some children, compared with others, bring extensive experience into school with them. But whether they do or not, children (who become Infants when they go to school, as Roger McGough points out in his poem 'Snipers') can only build on the foundations they have through the experiences they are offered in school. *The nature of those experiences is vital.*

Nor do the implications rest there. It is not only a matter of experiencing in the environment of the home what language is or can be used for, but also of imbibing fundamental attitudes through what is said, or left unsaid. It is from such everyday experiences that children construct what might be called a view of what is normal. They have never experienced anything else, and cannot know that there may be alternative versions of normalcy. On whether their construct coincides with or clashes with that held by school and teacher may depend their chances of success within the system.

There is now ample research evidence pointing to the correlation between the sort of social grouping in which children grow up and their subsequent performance in school. It is observable and demonstrable that some children come to school better equipped to take advantage of schooling than others. This is not altogether, as was once thought, simply a matter of intelligence. There are other factors. Among them may be numbered the child's underlying attitude towards the idea of education itself, and the possibilities that it might appear to hold out, an environmentally conditioned attitude shaping the approach to school and response to its demands. Another is, as we have seen, the language that the child brings into school, what it sounds like, and what he or she has been used to doing with it. What the school thinks of the child's language, and how it transmits its thoughts to the child, is of the utmost significance. It should not matter what anyone else's language sounds like, so long as communication is taking place – and communication, it should be insisted, is always a two-way process. If there is less of a tendency than there used to be to make dismissive judgements on the sounds of other people's language, a greater willingness to understand that, if you devalue somebody's language, then you devalue them as human beings, where it still happens a barrier is being erected between the child and its language: between resource and potential. As Mac Kenzie Mac Bride so eloquently recognized in 1910, *access to education is being effectively denied*.

All linguistic activity has a part to play in the learning process, although the activities of reading and writing have traditionally been more highly valued within the system than talking and listening. Reading is seen as the chief means of gaining knowledge, writing as a means of demonstrating how much knowledge has been acquired. Linguistic studies have revealed that there is much more to it than that, but as the ability to write remains the key to success within the system, it is incumbent upon the system to see to it that all that is currently understood about the process of writing should be incorporated into the business of writing in school, with the aim of maximizing the individual's ability to handle the writing system. It is a matter of dubious morality for the educational system to be run in such a way as to guarantee relative failure for well over half of those subjected to it because the system is seemingly incapable of adapting itself to take account of the implications of thought and research.

The writing system is different from the sound system (which we acquire first) although obviously related to it, and deriving from the same linguistic resource within the individual. Learning to write entails learning to use one's language in a new way, in a different medium. There is no reason why anyone born with a normal brain (and, as has been demonstrated, some with less than normal) into a language which possesses a writing system should not learn to write, and write adequately. Some take to this medium more easily, more quickly than others, for reasons which we do not yet understand, just as we do not understand why some are born more musical, or more artistic, than others. But this does not mean that nothing can be done for those to whom writing does not, as it were, 'come naturally', just as creative teaching can do something for the colour-blind or tone-deaf. Much, it is certain, will depend upon what they are asked to write in school, and the sort of response they get from their teachers.

We have seen how Derek Morrell emphasized that, at the heart of the learning process, is a complex relationship between the 'experience, language and values which the pupils bring into school from their homes and neighbourhoods, and those which are imported by the teacher'. If learning is to take place, there has to be what he called 'a reciprocity of feeling between the teachers and the taught'. Without this, the curriculum would remain 'simply an idea in the minds of the teachers'. (He might have added, in the minds of politicians, civil servants and administrators, as well.) Both teachers and pupils would be going through the motions of 'scholastic activity'. The role of the teacher is, therefore, seen as vital. What teachers know, what they understand, and – most important of all – what they transmit to the pupil, both implicitly and explicitly, holds the key to their pupils' success or failure within the system.

One important finding of the APU's Language Monitoring Programme provides an illustrative example of what this means in practice.[2] It is that which says that the quality of a pupil's writing depends upon the nature of the task being attempted. In short, response may be said to show 'task-specific characteristics'. There is an interaction taking place between pupil and task which will determine how linguistic resources may be drawn upon in order to respond to the task. Among the factors coming into play are:

(a) How the pupil 'sees' the task – what it entails, its finished form.
(b) What the pupil believes about his/her own abilities as a writer.
(c) What the pupil believes to be the characteristics of performance that will gain the approval of the teacher.

It will be recognized at once that these touch very closely on the pupil–teacher relationship already discussed, for it is what the teacher believes that will have been transmitted to the pupil and influence what he or she believes. Response to questionnaires administered as part of the Language Surveys revealed that many pupils regard 'spelling and punctuation' (one category) and 'neatness' as the chief characteristics of good writing. If they believe this; if they have been told, week after week, that their spelling and punctuation is/are weak; and if they have never received any effective help to remedy the situation, then they will not rate very highly their chances of turning in a performance which will gain approval. They will, apart from anything else, hardly be motivated to try very hard.

Apart from beliefs about the characteristics of 'good writing', there is another significant element. How one 'sees' a writing task, and forms some notion of what is required, depends to some extent on experience of similar tasks, and how one has approached them. The view that a teacher takes of what might be regarded as productive, worthwhile writing tasks is, thus, clearly of some importance. There is some evidence, again noted in the APU Language Survey Reports, in their analysis of replies to questionnaires, that by the time they leave Junior School at age 11, pupils may already have learnt to see writing in terms of two categories: imaginative and factual. The former, thought to involve expressiveness and creativity, is valued more highly than the latter, seen as a mere passing on of information, a utilitarian exercise into which questions of form and style do not intrude. There can be little doubt that the 'creative writing' movement of the sixties had, in its day, a liberating effect on the kind of writing that was done in school, but, as is the way with movements of this kind, it went too far. In the name of 'creativity' pupils were encouraged to put immediately on paper their feelings and impressions, without regard for some features of the writing system, with this activity given status as the most worthwhile kind of writing. Something of this lingers on in the categorization adopted in the National Criteria, of writing in 'open' and 'closed' situations. The dichotomy obscures that fact that *all* writing involves the writer in choice – of what to say, and how to say it. Labels do not alter that situation, or make it any easier. They do not absolve the writer from the necessity of choice, which is not so much a matter of a *general* raid on the inarticulate, as of a *specific* raid on one's own linguistic resource, prompted and constrained by motivation, perception, belief in one's own powers, the kind of reaction one has been used to getting – and previous experience.

All this points to an overriding need for the English curriculum to provide a *range of opportunities for writing*, distributed across as wide a functional spectrum as possible, and involving, beside the act of writing, integration of all linguistic activities. The doing of small-group activities, for example, which require collaboration and consultation in the process of working towards a known outcome, has been shown to yield a number of linguistic dividends. Among them are:

(a) Communicating to, and with, a known audience for a defined purpose.

(b) The making of meaning in a variety of situations within the group context, whether it be asking questions, giving answers, making suggestions, discussing alternatives, expressing ideas, etc.

(c) Highlighting the value of tentativeness in the early stages, thus stressing the need for rewording in the course of exploring, adapting and reshaping ideas.

(d) Giving insight into the interrelationship between the talk and other forms of linguistic input and output, namely reading and writing.

(e) Promoting confidence in tackling new, or unfamiliar, tasks. This should be especially helpful in the approach to tasks required by employment, or education, after school.

If the end-product is to be in written form, then care should be taken to emphasize the necessity of drafting a piece of writing (perhaps several times) before it may be considered ready for editing into its final form. It was J.K. Galbraith who said, in his autobiography, that one could not be a good writer if one did not know how bad one's first drafts were. This may be compared with much of the writing done in school, without benefit of drafting, in response to a sort of pedagogic highwayman's 'Stand and Deliver' demand.

The approach to writing being called for here argues the need for a form of course-work at all levels, especially in the secondary school. The keeping of a file of drafts and finished products, with the pupil presenting a selection for end-of-year assessment, has many advantages over more traditional methods, as reflected in the symbolically named exercise book. This might contain a number of 'stand and deliver' pieces, proof-read in red ink by the teacher, with the usual comments at the end, interspersed with language or comprehension exercises, whose irrelevance to the writing process can be assessed by looking at any progress between the first piece of writing in the book and the last. The year's (even the term's) endeavours may then be crowned by an exam requiring the pupil to write, again on demand, and do a comprehension exercise, now invariably by means of multiple-choice questioning. This results in a mark, or grade, purporting to represent somebody's 'ability in English'.

Course-work, by contrast, enables the pupils to become involved in their own work, and their own development, and take responsibility for what ·they present for assessment. By focusing attention on presentation, which may entail drafting, pupils will be enabled to gain insight into the nature of the process, while teachers, liberated from the chore of mechanical marking that seems to have no discernible effect on pupils' progress, will have more time to intervene in, and respond to, their pupils' writing in a more productive way.

As far as public exams at the end of the fifth year are concerned, a programme of course-work begun, say, after the Christmas holidays in the fourth form, designed to allow pupils to present a collection of pieces by Easter of the fifth year for GCSE assessment would have advantages even beyond those noted above. Not least among these would be the possibility of individual assessment for individual collections, thus taking note of the APU's task-specific finding. A first assessment by the teacher, who is in the best position to recognize the quality of the work, and who would take into account the functional variety of the collection, would be followed by moderation through school and consortium procedures. These would certainly be adequate, on what would be impression marking by those familiar with what fourth and fifth year pupils might be expected to achieve, to distinguish pass/fail boundaries, with perhaps two grades of pass. This is, after all, exactly the same way in which pass and failure is assessed in first Degree examinations, or how theses submitted for further Degrees are considered to have reached the required standard. Why more Grades than this might be required of subject English in school is difficult to see, unless it is for the reason that Peter Dixon gives in his poem, 'Oh bring back higher standards':

> . . . So let's label all the good ones,
> we'll call them 'A's and 'B's –
> and we'll parcel up the useless ones
> and call them 'C's and 'D's.
> . . . . We'll even have an 'E' lot!

. . . an 'F' or 'G' maybe!!
. . . so they can know they're useless,
. . . and not as good as me.

If the desire is, genuinely, to enhance the learning chances of
more pupils, especially those who enter school at a comparative
disadvantage, any system which condemns the next generation
of pupils to the same ineffective teaching methods as its prede-
cessors because it fails to take note of linguistic arguments will
surely frustrate that desire.

7   'Wot's it all for?'

' 'Ullo, 'Arry o'Cock. Wot's it all for? Eh? Wot's it all
bloomin' well for?'

H.G. Wells, *The Food of the Gods*

The question has to be asked, however, 'Is there a genuine
desire to enhance the learning chances of *all* children within the
system?' What, in fact, is seen as the purpose of the education
system? The answers given to these questions rest, ultimately,
upon the view that one takes of one's fellow human-beings, of
their worth, of their place in the scheme of things. On the values
encoded in the answers will depend what kind of opportunities
your education system will provide – and to whom; what counts
as success within the system; and how much education beyond
the statutory provision is accessible to what proportion of young
people.

The Introduction to the first Black Paper complained about
schools which 'have increasingly swung away from the notion
(which characterizes secondary education) that education exists
to fit certain sorts of people for certain sorts of jobs, qualifica-
tions and economic roles, to the idea that people should develop
in their own way at their own pace.' It would not be difficult to
argue that, judging by the quality of leadership they have
offered, there have not been many in recent years particularly
well fitted for the roles that they have played in all areas of our
public life, although they came through the system well before the
alleged change had come about. However, the matter is too
important to be a subject for facile charge and counter-charge.

Ralf Dahrendorf, in a Reith Lecture some years ago, gave his definition of the purpose of education:

> The central task for education is not simply to produce spare parts for our economic process, but to develop human abilities by opening them up for varied choices rather than streamlining towards alleged requirements.

This not only reflects a particular view of human worth and human dignity, but also recognizes, in a way the editors of the Black Paper did not, by his use of the phrase 'alleged requirements', that, in a period of rapid technological change such as we are living through, it is virtually impossible to predict what people might be required to do by the end of the century. It is of some consequence for the individual, and for society, that education should seek to 'develop human abilities by opening them up for various choices'. The main intention of this book, resting upon the premise that language is the supreme channel through which that must be accomplished, has been to show how far we are, in pedagogic terms, from achieving it – even if the political will existed to try.

The claim that language, and the way in which it functions, is not properly regarded by those who have responsibility for education, or who have made it their business (in at least two senses), has furnished the starting-point of several chapters. The shape of the education service in a democracy such as ours (and we should be grateful for this) is not established by blueprint emanating from a central source, although pressures tending in that direction have begun to build up. Rather, it has evolved over time, changing in piecemeal fashion in response to various pressures – political, social and intellectual. Populations grow, and decrease, and distribute themselves differently. Climates of opinion are created, developments ensue. The meteorological metaphor is instructive. What combination of power and influence decides where the high, or low, pressure systems will locate themselves at any point in time? Who, or what (institutions, for example), will exercise the decisive influence?

The development of comprehensive schools is a typical story.

They grew as a reaction against the tripartite system set up by the 1944 Act, although the third element – technical schools – never grew as intended. The Grammar/Secondary Modern system which did develop falsified the hopes which were invested, after the war, in an idea that was supposed, above all, to offer choice to 'bright' children of whatever class. The realization was gradually borne in that what was being offered was failure to between 80 and 90 per cent of the school population, and that this was being virtually guaranteed from the age of 11. So arose a demand for schools which appeared to eliminate selection at 11-plus, a demand that developed first at the ideological level, and then at the institutional. Development was patchy. Local Education Authorities varied in their enthusiasm for the new idea, even after central government made it a requirement that schemes for comprehensive reorganization should be drawn up and submitted, so that quality of planning and investment of resources varied widely. Many comprehensives began by preserving within themselves the Grammar/Secondary Modern split which their existence was intended to obliterate. One Grammar School Head appointed to run a newly established comprehensive was soon heard to say that he regarded his school as a 'Grammar School with more than its fair share of naughty boys'. There were many factors contributing to the haphazard nature of the development.

Teachers tended to go teaching what they knew in the way to which they were accustomed. Subject teachers in secondary schools begin their careers with a body of knowledge in which they see their professional future invested. It assumes the importance of a territory to be protected, if necessary defended, against would-be predators. It is also likely that they will have come into the classroom imbued with the ideas of Piaget, who took language development to be an aspect of cognitive development, and thus see their roles very much as that of passers-on of knowledge, mere agents of transmission.

It used not to be uncommon for teachers of the so-called academic subjects to assume that this body of knowledge, with which they had been equipped through University and/or College, would sustain them for the whole of their teaching career.

If they were seen to be good at 'passing it on', they might hope for promotion within the territorial limits of their subject, until they found themselves, perhaps, as Heads of Department, in charge of all the teaching in the subject within the school. It is a fact, with which all those engaged in in-service training are familiar, that, if you want teachers in Secondary Schools to take part in new developments – new subjects, for example, or new teaching methods – you will do well to rely, in the first instance, on teachers who no longer regard their subject as their territory, because they have been promoted to a post, such as Year Head or Deputy Head, which transcends subject boundaries. Exceptions to this rule, which may seem paradoxical in view of one of the main arguments of the book, are English teachers, because 'their' body of knowledge, English Literature, is of a different kind from other bodies of knowledge. It does not have the same kind of intellectual foundation; it includes a larger element of subjectivity. This is, perhaps, as has been observed, why they persist in regarding Parts of Speech and rules of punctuation as a body of knowledge to be handed on.

If you want teachers to respond to the demands of large institutional changes, such as those occasioned by the change to comprehensive schools, or, more recently, the need to amalgamate schools in face of the declining school population, then in-service training on a large scale, and adequate resources must be provided. Whether they are, or not, requires political decisions, because it is politicians, at national and local level, who have responsibility for providing resources out of taxes and rates: where responsibility for funding is shared at different levels there is no promise of a tidy outcome.

This has been compounded by a lack of consensus on the answers to the issues raised at the beginning of the chapter. Any answer given has political overtones. Voices are heard calling for the 'depoliticization' of education. Such a call is either disingenuous, or rests upon ignorance of the true nature of education. Any system that you set up, whether it is one of selection at 11-plus, or of comprehensive schools, makes a political statement. To pretend otherwise; to argue that the system you yourself happen to prefer is somehow a-political, is less than honest. Elected politicians have every right to frame, and resource, the education service as they see fit, providing that they take care to assess, as far as may be possible, the implications of what they are seeking to do for all those in the system. What is not defensible is playing politics with education, that is, with the lives of children in school. This may be done in a number of ways. You may seek to occupy ground staked out by your political opponents, as Callaghan did in his Ruskin speech; or you may attack, or defend, certain kinds of institution, and the teaching that goes on within them, not for educational but for political reasons. Politicians are not always inhibited by lack of evidence or a defensible intellectual position when they wish to score political points. They may also find some spurious issue, like that of 'standards' or the 'pursuit of excellence', and use it to pillory a system of which they disapprove on other than educational grounds. This, of course, is not to suggest that either educational standards, properly defined and measured, or the pursuit of excellence, properly understood, in teaching, are unimportant. It is the political use made of them as issues that is objectionable, and this is not confined to politicians.

Academics, as in the Black Papers or in the *Salisbury Review*, adopt the same tactics, and with much less justification. They should, one might have thought, have been better equipped to appreciate the intellectual shortcomings of what they were doing; to understand, for example, that the collection of what they called 'articles, quotations and anecdotes' offered as illustrations in the first Black Paper revealed little but prejudice at an anecdotal level.

The same can be said of much that passes, in the popular press, as educational journalism. It is sometimes difficult to avoid the conclusion that some journalists comb through educational reports to find material for sensational, doom-laden headlines which purport to identify weaknesses in the system. In January 1985 a committee investigating the state of primary education in the ILEA published its conclusions. In one paper, on the following day, under the headline 20 PER CENT OF PUPILS UNABLE TO READ BY EIGHT, appeared this first paragraph:

One in five London eight-year-olds cannot read simple sentences with confidence, according to the chairman of a committee investigating primary education which reported yesterday.

This headline, it will be noted, is a simplification of what was already (if indeed it was couched in the terms reported) an over-simplified remark. Properly to understand what the chairman was saying, one would need to know what, in his terms, a 'simple sentence' was; under what conditions this apparent failure was identified (were pupils stumbling over sentences in a passage they were being asked to read aloud, or were they being asked to read decontextualized sentences?); and how this 'fact' relates to the general pattern of individual reading development.

We are left until paragraph 4 of the article to learn that, despite this failing, 'ILEA 11-year-olds had improved their reading achievement between 1978 and 1983, to slightly better than the national average', and until paragraph 15 to discover that, 'a quarter of ILEA's 131,000 primary school-children come from single-parent families and 50,000 of them speak one of 147 languages other than English at home.' The contents of these two paragraphs could have been used to present the findings of the report as something of a success story, or at least as a picture far removed from that suggested by the headline. But newspapers have their readership to think of, their constituency to nurse, in more overtly political terms, and particular readerships are likely to have their views of education shaped by sectional, or class, interests. They may have concluded that widening choice for many might entail limiting privilege for others; but want to cloak their resistance to change in educational, or quasi-educational, arguments. Headlines such as that quoted may be useful. Those who make education their business, in the sense of gaining a livelihood from it, might sometimes betray a concern for *all* the children in the system, try to see it as a whole, and use their knowledge to make positive suggestions based upon educational considerations.

Mention has already been made of the role of others who

make education their business, like educational publishers and examination boards. The role of the latter is particularly interesting and influential. The Boards linked to Universities were quite happy to operate a system of O- and A-Levels designed to produce an 'elite' for Higher Education at the expense of the majority, while that system found general favour. Now that it no longer does, they have been equally happy to create a new cottage industry devising criteria for graded tests, the difference being that those who worked in the original cottage industries knew what they were doing.

It would be difficult to imagine any other area of human endeavour in which a change of the magnitude implied by graded assessment would not have been preceded by a large scale feasibility study designed to answer two questions; is it desirable? is it feasible? Such a study would have taken due notice of what was being done in related areas, such as that of the APU Language Monitoring Programme. Instead, a number of Boards launched their own initiative, each apparently preferring to find its own way to – what?

When Schools Council was set up, it was hoped that it would provide a forum for informed discussion of such educational issues. Derek Morrell, one of its founders, said that he hoped that,

> historians would recognize three things as its distinguishing characteristics: first that it aimed to foster a new respect for evidence, rationally interpreted, as an aid to the making of educational choices; second that it attempted to blend evidence, rational thought and judgement in a consensus which was no longer static, or so slow-moving as to almost seem so, but constantly developing to embrace new forms of experience; and third a commitment to evaluation through the best available consensus of informed and carefully formulated judgement, applied with respect for the unique wholeness of human personality.

Schools Council is no more. In the light of the foregoing paragraph, its abolition takes on, perhaps, a symbolic significance, as notice of an intention to downgrade the part played in

educational decision-making by 'evidence, rationally inter-
preted' and to move away from a 'consensus . . . constantly
developing to embrace new forms of experience'. There would
seem to be little chance of a post-Copernican view of language
establishing itself in a climate like this. Its implications, even if
only partially understood, are too uncomfortable for those who,
while claiming to want to extend access and choice, seek all the
time to restrict it.

Many of the schemes currently being suggested – vouchers,
diverting resources to 'successful' schools, Direct Grant Primary Schools – would have the effect of further weighting the
scales against those less culturally endowed by their background. In other words, any attempts to bring so-called 'market
forces' into education would inevitably lead to diminution of
chance for those in greatest need.

Moves to give greater power and influence to these who, after
the pupils themselves, have the greatest legitimate interest in
what goes on in schools, namely their parents, would have the
same effect. Parental views of education derive from a number
of sources. There is, first, their own experience of schooling, or
what they remember of it, and what they think it did for them.
Then there is what they believe to be the attributes of a good
schooling. Such beliefs invariably concentrate on surface features – homework, marking, and so on. As Parents' Evenings
regularly reveal, parents as a category hold the same folk-
linguistic and folk-pedagogic notions as the rest of society. In
this, they may be reinforced by the interventions of those whom
they wrongly suppose to be experts. Thus, when half a dozen
professors of engineering write to *The Times*[2] to express their
concern 'at the near-collapse in our schools' teaching of the
syntax of English', it might be supposed that, because they are
professors, they must know what they are talking about when
they write on the question of the teaching of grammar, and *The
Times* sees fit to print the letter. Parents are not to know that,
when it comes to matters linguistic, professors of engineering (or
of anything else) are likely to be as ignorant as the next man, as
pre-Copernican. It is to be hoped that they use a more scientific
approach, are less cavalier with the evidence, within the

boundaries of their chosen disciplines than they are outside them. It appears that an education system which conceives of learning in terms of mastering territories of knowledge does not always succeed in inculcating habits of intellectual rigour which carry beyond the frontiers of a particular subject.

But whatever their beliefs, and whatever foundation these may have, it will be the most articulate parents who will seize for their children the opportunities offered. This means, in effect, that, looked at from a social, or socio-economic, perspective, access to further and higher education will continue to be restricted to the same segment of the population as hitherto. Given the failure of this small pool of ability to supply a necessary range of developed ability in a hi-tech society, it is essential to give much greater access to the educational process in the early stages, and far more choice in the latter, so that a richer variety of talents may have a chance to develop.

The point was made recently, in a letter to the *Guardian* by an American Professor of English, Kenneth R. Johnson, that

in Japan and America, over 20 per cent of the adult work force has completed some course in higher (or tertiary level) education; in Britain, the figure is about 7 per cent. In the United States about 75 per cent of the nation's 18-year-old complete high school (a four-year programme) every year, and nearly half of these go on to some form of college education. In Britain, about 75 per cent of the nation's 16-year-olds leave school every year, and only about half of the remaining 25 per cent who go into the sixth form are able to enter college two years later. In other words, approximately 36 per cent of American 18-year olds go to college every year, compared with about 12 per cent of British 19-year olds; three times as many.

He goes on to argue that 'Study after study . . . shows that the most reliable educational variable in predicting a state's economic prosperity is its retention rate, i.e. the number of years children stay in school.'

Earlier in the book, it was pointed out that language has a two-fold aspect, individual and social. So, too, does education.

It is something of vital (in its literal sense) concern to the individuals who make up society, and to the well-being, present and future, of society itself. A book which began by asking why it is that a pre-Copernican view of language still holds sway in the intellectual life of our society has ended by having to ask questions about the whole of education, its nature and purpose; about the system which provides it; and about the climate which surrounds it. This is not surprising. Language and education are inextricably bound up together, because language is at the heart of the educational process. On an individual's opportunities to develop his/her own language primarily depend his/her learning chances.

A system tainted with misconceptions about the nature of language which have, on the one hand, the effect of denying respect for the individual's language, and, on the other, of maintaining an ineffective pedagogy, can succeed only in handicapping the chances of substantial numbers of the school population. They are prevented from gaining access to what is, in any case, a comparatively restricted range and depth of choice. This means, in effect, that the system is conniving at the creation, within a society in which the fruits of success are more openly displayed than ever before, of an element which increasingly feels that it has no chance of achieving what many would regard as no more than legitimate aspirations. It may be that society will eventually pay a heavy price for this, in one way or another.

When my great-great-grandfather reached Backbarrow in 1815, he found himself in a place in which boys and girls from the age of seven worked fourteen hours a day, standing at their machines from 5 a.m. to 8 p.m., with two half-hour breaks for meals. On Sundays they cleaned their machines from 6 until 12. This we know from the testimony of a former apprentice-master to a House of Commons Select Committee.[2] When it became generally acknowledged that this was not an acceptable way of treating young children, it was stopped by using the law to inject a moral element into the so-called 'ethics' of the market-place.

Some moral commitment is required to education. What Professor Johnson, in the letter already quoted, described as 'social Darwinism' is not good enough. While you cannot, in any system, see to it that some do not start at a disadvantage compared with others, what you can do it to give those do start at a disadvantage the best possible chance to catch up. We do not do enough, and nothing that has been so far proposed will substantially alter the situation for the better. We might make a start by approaching the problem from a respectable intellectual position.

References

Introduction
1 'The Relevance of Linguistics for the teacher of English' –
   Programme in Linguistics and English Teaching
   (Longman, 1968)

Chapter 1
1 Frank Palmer, *Grammar* (Penguin, 1971)
2 J. Honey, *The Language Trap* (National Council for
   Educational Standards, 1983)

Chapter 2
1 Joyce Cary, *The Horse's Mouth*
2 Gordon Wells, *The Meaning Makers* (Heinemann New
   Hampshire, 1985)
3 'Coursework Assessment in GCSE' (Secondary
   Examinations Council, Working Paper 2)

Chapter 4
1 M.A.K. Halliday, *An Introduction to Functional Grammar*
   (Edward Arnold, 1985)
2 David Mackay, Brian Thompson, Pamela Schaub,
   Breakthrough to Literacy (Longman, 1970)

Chapter 5
1 *Times Educational Supplement*, 19.12.1969
2 Brian Simon, *Does Education Matter?* (Lawrence & Wishart,
   1985)
3 A.B. Clegg, *The Excitement of Writing* (Chatto & Windus,
   1967)

Chapter 6
1 Peter Doughty, John Pearce, Geoffrey Thornton, *Language in Use* (Edward Arnold, 1971)
2 See Geoffrey Thornton, 'APU Language Testing 1979–83: An Independent Appraisal of the Findings' (DES, 1986)

Chapter 7
1 *Times Educational Supplement*, 19.12.1969
2 *The Times*, 25.2.1986
3 Quoted in E. Royston Pike, *Human Documents of the Industrial Revolution* (Allen & Unwin, 1966)

A note on reading

Other volumes in the Explorations in Language Study series address themselves to particular aspects of the general argument. In addition, the following may be found helpful:

Edwards, A.D., *Language in Culture and Class* (Heinemann Educational Books, 1976)

Gannon, P. and Czerniewska, P., *Using linguistics* (Edward Arnold, 1980)

Keen, J., *Teaching English: a linguistic perspective* (Methuen, 1978)

Stubbs, M., *Language and Literacy* (Routledge & Kegan Paul, 1980)

Appendix

Teaching the use of full-stops through definitions of a sentence involving terms like 'finite verbs' is not effective. Exploring patterns of language by some of the following methods has, on the other hand, been shown, in practice, to work.

1. A study of the way in which intonation is used, in speech, to give meaning. Thus, the linguistic structure 'Brian is coming' may be a question, a statement or even a command according to the intonation pattern. See *Teaching Writing*, pp. 49–52, for further suggestions as to how the concept of 'completeness' may be explored.

2. Transcribing speech into writing is a useful way of focusing attention on the differences between the two systems. Record part of a discussion, and select for transcription (in small groups) a short extract. (See, for more ideas, Healy, M., *Your Language* (Macmillan) Book One, pp. 33–4.)

3. A study of notices and advertisements (a Polaroid camera may be used to make a local collection) to see how layout, and different type-faces, indicate to the reader how words go together in groups.

4. Exploring the structure of sentences by playing Shannon's Game, in which, starting simply with a number of dashes equal to the number of words in a sentence which only the teacher knows, pupils are asked to guess and predict what the words are. See Unit D2 of *Language in Use*. Choose sentences which will emphasize those ways in which we learn how to predict that the end of a sentence is coming.

5. Games in which small groups build up sentences word by

word, and stories sentence by sentence. These can be recorded and transcribed.

6. Using as a basis for discussion passages to which an adapted form of Cloze procedure has been applied. Instead of deleting every tenth word, delete the words, or word groups, which end sentences.

7. Reassembling a poem which has been cut up into lines, so that pupils have to use syntactic, semantic and typographical clues to put it together again.

8. Discussing, in small groups, and rewriting pieces of writing which may cause difficulty to a reader. (An overhead projector is very useful for whole class discussion of particular points.) They need not necessarily cause such difficulty as the following, written by a twelve-year-old boy in a Remedial Department, the meaning of which is, with effort, accessible.

> Farman is wer you have crops and you neb pllt land for the crops and soive the RON seats in the soville and you have pllows to pllow the fallebs and you nebe gotelle to yete and the cows can gave melk